100 READINGS THROUGH
THE WORLD'S MOST IMPORTANT BOOK

THE ESSENTIAL BIBLE GUIDE

WHITNEY T. KUNIHOLM

The Essential Bible Guide
PUBLISHED BY WATERBROOK PRESS
12265 Oracle Boulevard, Suite 200
Colorado Springs, Colorado 80921

13 Digit ISBN 978-0-87788-074-5

Printed in the United States of America
2008

10 9 8

For Anna, Matthew, and Stephanie

Contents

Introduction

The Essential Bible Guide

"I've tried to read the Bible,
but I've never made it all the way through."

"I've read bits and pieces of the Bible,
but I don't really know how they all fit together."

"I've never read the Bible,
but I'd be interested to find out what's in it."

"I love the Bible. I just need a little
help understanding how it applies to my life today."

—Comments about the Bible

The Bible is the world's most important book. It has sold more copies than any other volume in history. It is the reference point for both the Jewish and Christian religions. And it has affected the culture, law, art, morality, and behavior of nearly every society on earth.

But the Bible is more than just an influential book. It is the historical record of the most important story of all time: God's interaction with humankind. Although the Bible contains many different styles of writing and introduces us to a wide variety of characters, everything in it combines to tell one main story: God created the world, humans rebelled against God, and God initiated a plan to save the world—a plan that culminated in Jesus Christ. That's the "Big Story" that makes sense of the Bible and all of life.

The Essential Bible Guide is your tool for discovering the Big Story for yourself. It leads you through one hundred easy-to-read passages—The Essential 100—and organizes them into twenty sections so you'll see how all the pieces fit together. Along the way it gives you many opportunities to record your insights and come to your own conclusions about how the Bible's message applies to you today—how your story connects to the Big Story.

FOLLOW THE BIG STORY

Before you get started on your journey through the Bible, it may help to have a road map. So here's a brief description of how the twenty sections in your study fit into the Big Story, God's plan of salvation.

The Old Testament

In the Beginning. The Bible introduces us to its main character—God—in the very first sentence of Genesis. God's first action is to create a beautiful and intricate world into which he places human beings made "in his own image." Unfortunately, it doesn't take long for the first humans, Adam and Eve, to sin and become separated from God. That sets up life's greatest dilemma: How can sinful men and women be reconciled to a holy God?

Abraham, Isaac, and Jacob. Fortunately, God takes the initiative for solving the dilemma. His first step is to form a group of people with whom he could begin a relationship. The three men in this section, sometimes called the patriarchs, are the ones God used to give birth to this special group of people, the Israelites.

The Story of Joseph. The Bible spends a long time on the story of this one man and his family. At first it appears as though God's plan to create a special nation has been derailed when Joseph is sold as a slave and taken away to Egypt. But it is in Egypt that "the Chosen People" grow from a small family into a great nation.

Moses and the Exodus. Eventually the Egyptians begin to oppress the Israelites, so God raises up Moses to lead his people to freedom. Throughout this process God demonstrates his awesome power and teaches the people some important lessons about trusting and obeying him. The Exodus also becomes a symbol of a greater freedom God would offer to all people—freedom from the bondage of sin.

The Law and the Land. Moses leads the people out of Egypt through the desert and brings them to the very edge of the Promised Land—a land God had promised years earlier to give Abraham's descendents. But it is Joshua who finally leads the people across the Jordan River into the land of Canaan. Along the way God reveals how he wants his people to live by giving them the Ten Commandments.

The Judges. The Israelites have now become a nation and have entered the Promised Land, but they have no king. Instead, God raises up interim leaders called judges, whose main responsibility was to save the people from the enemies surrounding them. As we read these exciting accounts, we see the consequences of disobedience as well as God's response when his people cry out and return to him.

The Rise of Israel. God eventually gives Israel a king, Saul, who starts well but in the end is rejected by God for being disobedient. Saul is succeeded by David, the shepherd boy who defeated a giant and became a national hero. As a result of David's military victories and spiritual passion, Israel reaches a high point in its history, and King David becomes a symbol of a much greater King to come, Jesus Christ.

The Fall of Israel. Although King Solomon is remembered for his wisdom and his incredible achievements, he also opened the door—just a little—to idolatry at the end of his reign. Over time this small compromise causes the people of Israel to wander far away from God and worship the false gods of the surrounding nations. Israel's idolatry leads to a devastating punishment—the destruction of Jerusalem and exile of the people to a foreign land.

Psalms and Proverbs. Psalms is a book of prayer and praise written mostly by David. As such, it provides a window into the inner life of a person whom the Bible describes as "a man after God's own heart." Proverbs is a collection of sayings, primarily of Solomon, that contain practical wisdom for living a godly life.

The Prophets. Throughout the history of Israel, God sends prophets who have the difficult task of pronouncing judgment on the idolatry and sin of the people. The prophets also predict the coming of a Messiah. As the Old Testament comes to a close, we are still waiting for the most wonderful part of God's plan to unfold.

The New Testament

The Living Word. What God had been saying through the history of Israel, through signs and wonders and through the Law and the Prophets, he now says in person. As the apostle John said, "The Word became flesh and made his dwelling among us" (John 1:14). Jesus Christ is a living, breathing statement of God's love for the world.

The Teachings of Jesus. Jesus communicates his message to the crowds using sermons and stories (parables). In his most famous sermon, the Sermon on the Mount, Jesus builds on the Law of Moses and explains with incredible insight how God intends for us to live. And in the parables, Jesus memorably explains one of the central themes of his teaching: the kingdom of God.

The Miracles of Jesus. The four gospels record many of Jesus' miracles. During his public ministry, he heals the sick, overrules the laws of nature, casts out demons, and raises the dead. His miracles not only demonstrate his compassion and power, but they also prove that he is who he claims to be: the Son of God.

The Cross of Christ. Jesus' main reason for coming to earth is to pay the penalty for sin and to offer salvation to all who believe in him. He accomplishes this by his death on the cross and his resurrection from the dead. The Cross of Christ is at the heart of God's plan of salvation. It is the way he resolves "the great dilemma" and enables any person to have a relationship with him. That's the Good News!

The Church Is Born. After Jesus' resurrection, he returns to heaven but sends a "greater gift," the Holy Spirit. This event marks the birth of the church. In addition, it initiates a dramatic expansion in God's plan of salvation. Ever since the time of Abraham, God has been relating to one group of people, the Israelites. But now the door of salvation is open to everyone.

The Travels of Paul. The most energetic ambassador of the early church is the apostle Paul. Originally, Paul was a bitter enemy of the church, but God dramatically turns him around on the Damascus road and transforms him into a fearless witness for Christ. Paul's missionary journeys, recorded in the book of Acts, are a major reason why the gospel begins to spread throughout the world.

Paul to the Churches. Paul writes many letters to the new believers in the churches he has started. In them he explains the gospel, encourages believers to grow in their relationship with God, and offers practical help for living the Christian life.

Paul to the Leaders. Paul knows that if the church is to grow, it will need capable leaders to carry on after him. Therefore, he writes some of his letters to instruct church leaders and to warn against false teachers. Since the church is the way God will continue expanding his plan of salvation in the world until Jesus returns, faithful leadership in these new churches is vitally important.

The Apostles' Teaching. In addition to Paul, other apostles such as Peter, James, and John write letters to encourage and instruct the early followers of Jesus. Each of these letters helps us understand new facets of the gospel and the Christian life. They also provide us with some of the most memorable passages in the Bible.

The Revelation. Near the end of his life (around A.D. 95), the apostle John has a spectacular vision. Through it, God reveals specific messages to seven first-century churches. These messages are still highly applicable to churches in the twenty-first century. In John's vision, God also foretells and describes Christ's return, when God's plan of salvation—the Big Story—will reach its ultimate fulfillment.

HOW TO USE *The Essential Bible Guide*

The Essential Bible Guide takes you through the Bible in one hundred readings, with five readings per section. The readings are not dated, so you can complete them at any pace, although completing one reading a day or five each week would be the best way to get a meaningful overview of the Bible.

This guide is designed to be used with a Bible. I recommend that before you begin your study, you find a Bible that is easy for you to read. Although the *King James Version* is a beautiful and widely available translation, it is often difficult for modern readers to understand since it was translated into seventeenth-century English. For this reason, I recommend that you use one of the many excellent modern translations such as the *New International Version* (NIV), the *New Living Translation* (NLT), or the *Contemporary English Version* (CEV). If you are still unsure about which Bible translation to use, you might want to check with a minister or priest.

You will notice that each study follows a five-step format—Pray, Read, Reflect, Apply, Pray—that you can use anytime you read the Bible. In the Bible God speaks to you. In prayer you can respond to him. So by integrating the two, you can have a regular dialogue with God.

Here's what to do in each of the five steps:

1. **PRAY** before you read the Scripture passage, asking God to help you understand his Word. The written prayer will get you started, but feel free to add thanksgiving, confession, praise, or whatever you'd like to express to God. Remember, you're beginning a conversation.
2. **READ** the Bible passage carefully. If you have time you may want to read the passage more than once or review the surrounding passages for context. Keep a pencil or highlighter handy so you can make notes or underline key phrases or verses.
3. **REFLECT** on what you've read. First, summarize your own observations of the passage in the space provided. It may help to ask yourself, What was the main point of this passage? Which verses relate

to my life now? Then think further about the passage by reading the commentary.

4. **APPLY** to your life what God teaches you from his Word. Take some time to think this through. Did the passage contain an example to follow, a warning to heed, a promise to claim? How should this affect your thoughts, words, and actions? In the space provided, jot down how you'd like to apply these things in your life.
5. **PRAY** again, asking God to help you live out his Word. This time turn the things you've learned into prayers. Also pray about your own needs and the needs of others. And be sure to thank God for any answers to prayer.

At the back of the book, you'll find a **Review Journal**. This is your opportunity to summarize your most significant insights from the five readings and to prioritize the main ways you'd like to apply what you learned from the Bible. Before you begin a new review, take time to read what you've written in the previous reviews. By doing this you'll get a clearer picture of what God is saying to you on your journey through his Word.

A GROUP CHALLENGE

Some people find it more encouraging to read the Bible in a group. Your church may want to make *The Essential Bible Guide* a congregation-wide challenge, led by the pastor and other church leaders. Or, if you are part of a Bible study or home group, you might suggest that your group read through this study together. Whatever method you use, reading *The Essential Bible Guide* as a group will enable you to compare your experiences and encourage one another. You may even want to read through this study with your family or with colleagues at work, where you can compare your insights via e-mail.*

---

* For more ideas on using The Essential 100 as a group event, see page 267.

YOUR HIGHER GOAL: MEETING GOD

The thirty-nine books of the Old Testament and the twenty-seven books of the New Testament were written by many authors over a fifteen-hundred-year time span. Yet each author was uniquely inspired by God. As the apostle Paul said, "All Scripture is inspired by God and is useful to teach us what is true" (2 Timothy 3:16, NLT). The apostle Peter said, "For prophecy [the Bible] never had its origin in the will of man, but men spoke from God as they were carried along by the Holy Spirit" (2 Peter 1:21). And Jesus emphasized this truth when he quoted from Deuteronomy, "It is written, 'Man shall not live by bread alone, but by every word that proceeds from the mouth of God'" (Matthew 4:4, RSV).

What distinguishes the Bible from any other book is its divine origin. That's why people often refer to it as God's Word; it records what he's said, what he's done, and what he wants from us.

So as you begin your journey through the one hundred essential passages from the Bible, remember that your goal is not just to read the world's greatest book or to gain more Bible knowledge or even to develop greater spiritual discipline. All those things are important, but your higher goal is to meet the Author. The secret to making Bible reading more than just a good habit is to think of it as an opportunity to meet God every day, to have a daily encounter with the God who made you, who loves you, and who desires to have a living relationship with you.*

My prayer is that over the next few months, the Bible and its timeless message will come alive for you as never before. But don't let these readings be the end of your journey in the Bible. Let this study become the beginning of a lifetime adventure of meeting God daily in the Bible and through prayer.

---

* If you'd like to know more about how you can discover a lifetime relationship with God, see page 264.

Part I

OLD TESTAMENT

In the Beginning

If you really want to understand something, you need to go back to the beginning. For example, if you want to develop a serious relationship with another person, you want to find out where he came from, how he grew up, and what he did before you met. Or if you want to buy a house, you first find out when it was built, what special features were part of the original design, and how the property has been maintained over the years.

But if you want to understand where the world came from or, for that matter, where human beings came from, where can you go? That's where our first five readings can help. They describe the creation of the world, the "birth" of humankind, and the beginning of civilization. It makes for some interesting reading.

The Bible begins with arguably the most famous opening sentence ever written: "In the beginning God…" It makes no apology for this fundamental assertion: *God exists*. That's the truth upon which the entire book and all of life are based. You can read the Bible as history, or you can read it as literature. Certainly, it is both. But ultimately, the Bible is a book about God, and that's what makes it unique.

Another feature of these five readings is that they introduce us to a number of "firsts." We read about the first humans, the first sin, the first guilty conscience, and the first case of pride. Because we are reading about the beginning of time and human history, everything is a first. But even though it all happened many years ago, the themes have a very contemporary ring.

It's worth considering one other first from these readings, God's first recorded words: "Let there be light" (Genesis 1:3). As you work through this book, you'll discover that God's intention has always been to shine his light into the darkness. He did this in the most incredible way by sending his own son, Jesus Christ, to die on the cross and break the power of darkness once and for all.

But we're getting ahead of ourselves. There are some important things we need to learn about God, the world, and ourselves first. So our journey through the Bible needs to start at the beginning. And that's where we're about to go.

Reading 1

MEET THE AUTHOR

PRAY

Heavenly Father, thank you for this opportunity to spend time with you. Please "open my eyes that I may see wonderful things in your law" (Psalm 119:18).

READ GENESIS 1–2.

REFLECT

Right from the start the Bible introduces us to its main character: "In the beginning God…" (1:1). The rest of this wonderful book is all about him. Theologians describe the Bible as God's "self-revelation." This means it's not only a book *about* God, it's also a book *by* God. He inspired the human writers (2 Peter 1:21; 2 Timothy 3:16). So if you want to meet God, read his Book.

Next, the Bible tackles one of life's biggest questions: How do we explain the origins of the universe? Some scientists look in the dirt for answers. But the Bible looks to the heavens (1:1). Of course, science does have its place in helping us explore the natural world. But to truly explain it, we must accept that God made it, and today's reading gives us two perspectives on how he did it.

1. *The big picture* (1:1–2:3). As we read this overview of the seven days of Creation, we notice that God took the initiative. He didn't just sit back and wait for life to emerge from the ooze. He had a plan and a design for his world. Experiences such as holding a newborn

baby or looking at the stars on a clear night are evidence for what an incredible design it was.

2. *The human interest story* (2:4-25). Genesis 2:4 is like a hyperlink to more information on a key part of the story—the creation of humankind. We've already learned that God chose to make men and women and that both reflected his image (1:27). Now we learn that human beings possess at least two other distinctives: God's life (2:7) and God's standards (2:16-17). We have a God-given conscience, an innate sense that there is such a thing as right and wrong. To live as if it were not so is inhuman.

APPLY

In what ways do you see evidence for God in the world around you? When do you feel closest to God?

PRAY

Thank you, Lord God, for the incredible design and beauty of your creation. Help me do a better job of caring for it...

Reading 2

EYES WIDE OPEN

PRAY

Lord, I'm grateful that you've given us the Bible and that I have the freedom to read it. Help me understand your word to me today…

READ GENESIS 3.

REFLECT

Popular culture sometimes portrays sex as "the original sin." But that's not what the Bible says. The joy of sexual intimacy between a husband and wife is part of God's design for creation (Genesis 2:23-25). Rather, the original sin was to question (3:1), challenge (3:4), and then disobey (3:6) God's definition of right and wrong (Genesis 2:16-17). Both Adam and Eve made that tragic mistake, and it has affected all of creation ever since. We only have to read history or, if we are honest, look at our own lives to see this is true.

Sin brought immediate consequences. For Eve it meant increased pain in childbirth and a new strain in her relationship with her husband (3:16). For Adam, sin meant pain in his work and futility in his life (3:17-19). Can you imagine what it would be like if our relationships were always satisfying and our work was always meaningful?

But the biggest consequence of sin was not just that it warped God's perfect creation. It broke our relationship with God. Adam and Eve had enjoyed a unique and close fellowship with God (3:8-9), but now they became afraid of him and tried to hide (3:10). As we read about how they began to rationalize their behavior, we witness the introduction of *guilt* into the world (3:11-13). Finally, Adam and Eve were banished from God's presence with no way to get back (3:23-24).

Pain, sorrow, futility, guilt, difficulty in relating to others, separation from God. What a horrible predicament sin has placed us in. But the Good News is that God had a plan to solve that problem—a plan that would culminate in Jesus Christ. And that's what the rest of the Bible is all about.

APPLY

What makes you feel guilty? Have you done anything recently that you regret? If so, how could you make things right with others and with God?

PRAY

Dear Lord, it's hard for me to admit it, but I have a problem with sin. Please forgive me and help me live in a way that pleases you...

Reading 3

Wipe Out!

Pray

Heavenly Father, I have so many things on my mind and heart today. Help me set them aside so that I can spend focused time with you…

Read Genesis 6:5–7:24.

Reflect

In our last reading we saw how human beings decided to leave God's path and go their own way. The Bible calls that decision *sin,* and in this passage we see how far from God sin will take us (6:5). It's the nature of sin that it always gets worse. It grows like cancer. Left unchecked, it will destroy us. So we can understand why God is so upset when we sin. It's hard to let someone you love make bad choices.

Some people think that God is just waiting to catch them doing something wrong, as if he enjoys punishing people. But it's interesting that his first emotion here is not satisfaction or even anger. Rather, it is pain and grief (6:6-7). That's what our sin does to the heart of God. And as we've learned, sin brings horrible consequences that eventually force God to act—like a potter who is working with a lump of flawed clay and decides to start over.

We again hyperlink to the story of Noah (6:9–7:24), a man who lived in contrast to the sin and violence all around him. Why was God so pleased with Noah? Because Noah was willing to listen to and obey God's word

(6:22; 7:5). That's the definition of righteousness. And think about the phrase, "after the seven days" (7:10). We can only imagine how Noah felt during that week. Even so, he obeyed God when it made no sense and there were no visible results. God is still pleased with that kind of faith.

The flood temporarily wiped out the sin-prone culture of that day (7:22-23), but it was not to be the end of the world. Even as God unleashed this overwhelming judgment of sin (7:17-24), he promised a new beginning (6:18). In spite of the dark clouds, we get another hint that God has a plan for the salvation of the world.

Apply

Do you find yourself in situations where you are surrounded by sin? How could you respond in ways that are pleasing to God?

Pray

Lord God, I want to follow your way for my life. Please help me keep my eyes on you and your path, no matter what those around me are doing...

Reading 4

NEVER AGAIN

PRAY

Heavenly Father, I worship and praise you. Please give me a greater sense of your presence as I read your Word today...

READ GENESIS 8:1–9:17.

REFLECT

We used to have a beagle named Rascal. He was pretty high-strung, and whenever I'd open the door to take him for a walk, he'd go berserk and bolt for the open lawn, scraping my knuckles and the leash against the screen door. So I can easily imagine the joyous eruption that is captured in Genesis 8:18-19. Free at last!

But were they? Yes, Noah, his family, and the animals were free from that smelly ark, but were they really free from the stench of sin? Had the flood wiped that slate clean? As we will quickly see in our readings through the Bible, the answer is a very definite and sad no.

Noah seems to understand this underlying dilemma. That's why his first act was not to party; it was to worship (8:20). God is pleased when we humbly seek him (8:21-22). Noah's response to God also hints at one of the great themes in the Bible: sacrifice as a way of seeking forgiveness for sin. We'll see this theme developed throughout the Old Testament, and when we get to the New Testament, we'll discover it's the key for understanding the death and resurrection of Jesus Christ.

Of course, God understands the reality of sin all too well, but that's what makes his promise to Noah all the more poignant (9:8-17). "Even though" God knows human beings are hopeless sinners (8:21), "never again" will he consider completely destroying them (8:21; 9:11,15). In fact, he would go to great lengths to assure them that his intent was to do just the opposite. At this point in history, a rainbow became the symbol of his love. But before long he would come down to earth and say it in Person.

APPLY

What things remind you most powerfully that God loves you? What's one creative thing you could do today to show God you are grateful for his love?

PRAY

Dear Lord, thank you for loving me even though you know all the secrets of my heart...

Reading 5

CAN WE TALK?

PRAY

What a joy it is to meet with you, Lord. Help me quiet my heart and mind so I can hear your still, small voice today…

READ GENESIS 11:1-9.

REFLECT

What was so bad about the Tower of Babel? After all, jobs were being created, people were working together for a common purpose, technological progress was being made, and society seemed to be on the verge of a lasting achievement. A track record like that would get any politician elected today. So what was the problem?

Perhaps we get a clue in verse 4. The driving motivation for all this seemingly good work was to gain *human* glory rather than God's glory. And here we confront what C. S. Lewis called "the worst of all vices"—pride. Ever since Adam and Even committed the first sin, humans had increasingly chosen to go their own way instead of God's. This fantastic tower became a defiant human statement: "*We're* in charge here." But they weren't; God was still the Creator and Lord of all. That's why he confused and scattered the people of Babel (11:7-9). God won't let our unbridled pride continue forever (Proverbs 16:18).

At the same time God affirmed the power of good communication in the most incredible way (11:6). Imagine what could be accomplished in our political arenas, our workplaces, our churches, and especially our families if we were able to effectively communicate with one another while avoiding the power games of pride. Nothing would be impossible! But the sad truth is, pride is here to stay. And it's not just a problem for "them." Pride has infected us all.

In the end the tower didn't come crashing down. It was left standing on a deserted plain, a monument to the futility of trying to live without God. This story would have come to a much different conclusion if the people had followed Noah's example (Genesis 8:20-22). When we acknowledge and worship God, he can accomplish incredible things through us.

APPLY

Is there someone in your life with whom you have difficult or even broken communication? How has pride been a factor in that struggle? How could you change the situation?

PRAY

O Lord, no matter how hard I try, pride seems to sneak into my heart. Please forgive me and help me honor you in all that I do... *

---

* Now turn to the Review Journal beginning on page 253 to record your key insights from the last five readings. You'll see that space has been provided for you to journal after each section.

ABRAHAM, ISAAC, AND JACOB

The miracle of Creation and the beauty of the Garden of Eden were filled with promise. But as we've seen, once sin entered the world, everything took a turn for the worse. After less than a dozen chapters in Genesis, God has already had to punish all humankind by nearly wiping them out with a flood and then scattering them—like dropping a pebble on an anthill—for their pride at the Tower of Babel.

The world was unraveling, and the biggest problem was that humans couldn't do anything about it. Their only hope was that God would do something—and quick! That's why our next five readings are so important. They show us what God did—how he took the first step to save us. His plan was to create a great nation—Israel—and then through it to bless the whole world with a Savior. But only he could make the first move, and he did that by choosing one man, Abram—who he later named Abraham.

Abraham, his son Isaac, and his grandson Jacob are sometimes referred to as the patriarchs. They were the first building blocks in this great family of God. But as you'll see, they weren't perfect. They had weaknesses; they resisted God; they sinned. But God still used them. That should be an encouragement to us. God's plan isn't thwarted by our mistakes.

We may also wonder why God went to the trouble of reconciling us to himself. Why not just have another huge flood and be done with it? God decided not to because, as C. S. Lewis wrote in *The Screwtape Letters,* "He *really* loves the hairless bipeds He has created."

There's one more theme you'll want to keep an eye on in these readings: faith. That's the main thing Abraham did right. He didn't know why God had picked him, he didn't know where God was sending him, and he certainly didn't know what God's plan was. All he knew was that God said, "Leave," and so he did.

Trusting God with your life is what faith is all about. In the New Testament the apostle Paul explained that Abraham's example pointed to a bigger step of faith—to believe in Jesus Christ as Savior and Lord (Romans 4:16-25).

Reading 6

WHY ME?

PRAY

Heavenly Father, your Word is such an incredible gift. I ask that you would speak to me in some specific way through it today...

READ GENESIS 12.

REFLECT

Of all the people in the world, why did God single out Abram to receive such an incredible promise (12:2-3)? Our passage doesn't give us many clues, but it does remind us that God had a plan: He wanted to bless the whole world. The problem was, sin made it impossible for humans to fix their broken relationship with God and receive this blessing (Genesis 3:23-24). One of the most incredible truths about God is that he loves us so much that he took the initiative; he made the first move.

That's not to say we have no responsibility for developing a relationship with God—"If you want me to get saved, God, you know where to find me." Abram actively responded to God's initiative, and so should we. During his seventy-five years, Abram had apparently cultivated the habit of listening for God's voice. He was also willing to obey. When God said, "Leave," Abram left, even when the destination was unknown (12:1). And Abram didn't forget about God along the way; he frequently took time out to remember what God had done and to cultivate his relationship with him (12:7-8).

Abram is one of the great examples of faith in the Bible (Genesis 15:6; Romans 4). But that's what makes his reaction to the famine so curious (12:10). After all God had said and done, wouldn't you think Abram could trust God for food? Instead, Abram relocated to Egypt (note that God didn't tell him to go), and then he came up with a lame story to "protect" himself and his wife.

Even when we know what God wants us to do, we still mess up. The Good News is, God stays with us even when we make poor choices. We may have to face tough or painful consequences, but God never leaves us. In fact, he often uses the detours of our lives to teach us things we'd never learn otherwise.

APPLY

How did God find you? How have you responded to him? What detours have you encountered in your journey through life? What did God teach you through these experiences?

PRAY

Heavenly Father, thank you for making the first move to find me. I don't fully understand your love for me, but I'm so grateful for it. Help me listen for your voice and follow you every step of my journey…

Reading 7

HE FEELS YOUR PAIN

PRAY

Lord, you know the secrets of my heart. I begin this time by inviting you to show me the areas of my life that you want to fill with your presence...

READ GENESIS 15.

REFLECT

It must have been a nerve-wracking time for Abram. He was already well past retirement age when God told him to leave everything behind and head off to an unknown destination (Genesis 12:4). God doesn't always give us a detailed road map for life. Often he just shows us what to do next. Faith is trusting that God will get us to the right destination. Or, as preacher and author Oswald Chambers often said, "Trust God and do the next thing." But as we see in Abram's experience, having faith doesn't mean everything will be easy or will make sense.

A sensitive issue. The inability to have children was a cause for shame in ancient times, especially for women. It seems that God's amazing promise to build a nation had become the source of emotional pain for Abram and Sarai—"We don't even have one child yet!" (15:2-3). But God was using Abram's most sensitive point as an opportunity to build his faith (15:6).

What are you sensitive about right now? What do you fear the most?

Sometimes the only way to deal with our fear and pain is to honestly say, "God I hate this, and I need you to show me what you are trying to teach me."

An impossible task. Whenever we follow God's will, there comes a point when things look bleak. Abram found the land filled with "ites" (15:19-21). Now what? God knew that Abram needed encouragement, so he gave him a peek at the master plan (15:12-18). Don't you wish he'd do that for you? "God, if you'd just e-mail your plan in advance, that would really help." Actually, there's a sense in which God *has* revealed his plan to us. We get the clearest picture by reflecting on what he's done in the past—in the Bible and in our lives—and then trusting that he'll be faithful in the future. That's the best thing to do when things seem impossible.

God revealed his will to Abram and built Abram's faith. But the greatest thing God did was to let Abram experience his presence. Ultimately, it is a real experience of God that wipes away our fear, pain, and questions and enables us to go through anything in life with courage and joy.

APPLY

Are there any "ites" in your life—things that seem impossible to overcome? How could you respond in a way that shows your faith in God?

PRAY

Dear Lord, you know the things that cause me pain, anxiety, and worry. Show me how you are at work through those things, and help me trust you more…

Reading 8

STRANGE BUT TRUE

PRAY

Today I just want to praise you, heavenly Father. You are so awesome and good and loving to me. I want you to know how much I love you…

READ GENESIS 21:1–22:19.

REFLECT

We begin today's reading with a story so odd it could make headlines in the *National Enquirer:* Ninety-Year-Old Woman Pregnant…by One-Hundred-Year-Old Man! But this story is true, and it demonstrates once again that God can do the impossible, not only in the pages of the Bible but also in our lives. Since our last reading God has provided a personal reminder of his promise to build a nation by changing Abram's name, which means "exalted father," to Abraham, which means "father of many" (Genesis 17:5). It was a reminder Abraham would soon need.

The story gets odder still when God instructs Abraham to sacrifice his and Sarah's only son, Isaac (22:2). Any parent will immediately feel the horror of such a dilemma. But perhaps the most amazing part of the story is that Abraham wastes no time obeying God. "Early the next morning" he sets out (22:3). He doesn't argue or question God's intention this time. It took a lifetime, but Abraham learned to trust God no matter what. That's still the goal of the Christian life.

What Abraham couldn't see is that God was using what seemed like a cruel test to make a profound statement. As the tension mounts in front of the makeshift altar, Abraham unwittingly prophesies God's plan of salvation, "God himself will provide the lamb for the burnt offering" (22:8). Indeed, God did provide the Lamb, his only Son, Jesus Christ, who died on the cross, the once-for-all sacrifice for our sins. That's the Big Story in a nutshell. The Lamb of God is at the heart of the Good News.

It's true that God sometimes tests us, and it doesn't feel good when he does. But God's tests build our faith like nothing else can and produce blessing in our lives far greater than we'll ever be able to see at the time (22:15-18). And no matter what happens, we can trust that God's plan is the best thing for us (Romans 8:28).

APPLY

Is God testing you in some way at this time? Explain. How do you think God wants to build your faith through it?

PRAY

Heavenly Father, please open my eyes to what you are doing—and what you want me to learn—in the challenges I face today...

Reading 9

ANALYZE THIS!

PRAY

Heavenly Father, I thank you that you have invited me to be part of your family. Help me to live in a way that brings honor to you...

READ GENESIS 27–28.

REFLECT

A psychiatrist could have a field day analyzing Isaac's dysfunctional family. A permissive father, a controlling mother, an errant older twin, and a deceptive younger twin. Get them all fighting for the family inheritance, and—*hot dog!*—you have the plot line for a made-for-TV movie. But this is one of the most important families in the Bible because God used them to build the nation of Israel. So let's take a closer look at what's going on here.

In ancient times "the blessing" was an important way to pass on the wealth and leadership of a family. And from the way Isaac treated it, the blessing seemed to have some kind of spiritual impact as well (27:27-40). Blessing children is still important today. Parental affirmation is still one of our most basic needs as humans, and whether we receive it or not can either strengthen or weaken us for the rest of our lives. Children today are desperate for the love and acceptance of their parents, especially their fathers. When that's not possible, godly adults can have a huge positive impact by extending a blessing to the children in their circles of influence.

But the truth is, no family is perfect. God uses broken people to accomplish his purposes. He has no other choice. Take Jacob, for example. He let his mother manipulate him, he used a costume to steal his brother's blessing, and then he had to run for his life. But Jacob's failure isolated him so that God could deal with him in a personal way (28:10-22).

As painful as they may be, the broken parts of our lives are some of our best opportunities to have an encounter with the living God.

APPLY

What were the patterns, both healthy and otherwise, in the family you grew up in? How have these patterns shaped you today? What can you do to be a more godly influence in your family?

PRAY

Lord Jesus, I pray that you would draw my family members closer to you. Please show me how I can be part of what you are doing in their lives...

Reading 10

TRUE RECONCILIATION

PRAY

Dear Lord, thank you for accepting me. I love you and praise you this day. I want to learn everything you want to teach me…

READ GENESIS 32–33.

REFLECT

Sometimes guilt motivates people to do bad things, such as lying or covering up the truth with a new crime. Here's an example of guilt motivating someone to do a *good* thing. Jacob obviously had a guilty conscience. Years earlier he had deceived his brother, Esau, and had stolen both Esau's birthright and blessing. But Jacob's guilt eventually caused him to begin taking steps to patch things up with his brother.

But was it really reconciliation that Jacob was after? Probably not. Jacob was just hoping to save his own skin by flattering and paying off his brother (32:13-21). Even his prayer life had a guilty ring (32:11). True reconciliation first involves a change of heart and then a change of actions—that's repentance. Sometimes it takes a long time for God to change our hearts, mostly because it is so difficult for us to admit our sin. But until we do, we rationalize our actions instead of changing them, and we remain trapped by our guilt and sin.

Ironically, it was Esau who exhibited true reconciliation. Years earlier he was an "urge-driven" brute bent on getting even. But by the time he met Jacob again, he was a content man (33:9) who held no grudges and was willing to genuinely embrace his nervous brother. Esau is an Old Testament example of the loving father in the parable Jesus told many years later (Luke 15:11-32). The point is that God can reconcile our most broken relationships. But we must let him do it his way; we must be willing to change.

Sometimes life can make us become so guilt-ridden, bitter, or angry that the only thing that could change our hearts is a genuine experience of God. That's what happened to Jacob (32:22-32). If there are difficult relationships and situations in your life right now, maybe you need to stop asking God to change the circumstances. Instead, pray that God will help you understand and accept how he's trying use those circumstances to change you.

Apply

Think of a relationship in your life that is strained or broken. What might God be trying to teach you through it? In what way could you change to make things better?

Pray

Heavenly Father, you have welcomed me with open arms. Please help me show your all-embracing love, even to those who frustrate and irritate me... *

---

* Now turn to the Review Journal beginning on page 253 to record your key insights from the last five readings.

The Story of Joseph

Our next five readings will take us through the story of Joseph. As you will see, the Bible gives Joseph a lot of "air time." What's so important about this one man that fourteen chapters in Genesis are devoted to the ups and downs of his life?

For one thing, the story of Joseph forms an important bridge between the patriarchs (Abraham, Isaac, and Jacob) and Moses. Most people know the story of how Moses confronted Pharaoh and commanded him to "Let my people go." But it's the story of Joseph that shows us how and why the people of Israel landed in Egypt in the first place.

Another important point about Joseph's life is that it clearly demonstrates God's sovereignty—that is, his complete control over all things. No matter how bad the situation got for Joseph—and it got pretty bad—God was always using it for good (Genesis 50:20; Romans 8:28). That's an encouraging reminder when we face crises and disasters in our own lives today.

Perhaps the most significant aspect of the Joseph narrative is that it becomes the next chapter in the Big Story of the Bible, God's plan of salvation for all people. Years earlier God had told Abraham that his family would become a great nation and would be a blessing to the whole world. But at that point, Abraham's descendents were a motley bunch of nomads with a history of family problems. It looked like the famine would break up the family and put an end to the Big Story.

But God let Joseph and his brothers get into a jam so that he could demonstrate his willingness and ability to deliver his Chosen People. At this point in the Big Story, God delivered the people from famine and oppression

(Genesis 45:5-7). Later, God would accomplish a much greater deliverance from sin and death through the work of his Son, Jesus Christ. That was the great blessing God had in mind from the beginning, and that's what makes the story of this one man so important.

Reading 11

FAMILY FEUD

PRAY

Lord, I really enjoy having this opportunity to be in your presence. Please help me understand what I read and what you want me to do in response…

READ GENESIS 37.

REFLECT

It doesn't take a genius to figure out why Joseph's family had problems. As with most sibling rivalry, it's rarely the fault of just one person. When things go wrong, we tend to remember "the big blowup," but it usually takes some time for tensions to get to the boiling point. Let's take a look at what caused things to heat up in this family.

Favoritism. Joseph probably was a gifted child. But that was no excuse for his father to play favorites and rub it in with a conspicuous gift (37:3). In so doing, Jacob opened the door to a lot of bitterness. One of the most destructive things in a family is when "love" becomes a tool for manipulation or control.

Arrogance. Surely Joseph knew that no one likes a tattletale, especially older brothers (37:2). But he didn't seem to care. He even uses his spiritual experiences to tease his brothers (37:5-9). God has given each of us spiritual gifts. But to be used effectively, they must be combined with humility.

Jealousy. What bothered the brothers most is that they wanted what

Joseph had: their father's blessing (37:4,11). Imagine how different things would have been if Jacob had called a family meeting to say, "I love each one of you." Are there people in your family who need to know that you love them?

Hate. Three times this passage says that Joseph's brothers hated him (37:4,5,8). If we let our angry feelings go unresolved, they'll destroy us from the inside out. It's much better to follow Jesus' example (Matthew 5:43-48; 18:15-17) and deal with the little offenses before they fester into full-blown hate.

APPLY

What causes tension and conflict in your family? How could you express genuine love to the ones who need it most?

PRAY

Heavenly Father, I'm so thankful that you love me. Help me to truly love the people around me, especially those in my family...

Reading 12

NO FAIR!

PRAY

Lord, you have been so good to me. Thank you for the many ways you have blessed me. I especially thank you for this time with you, reading your Word to me...

READ GENESIS 39–41.

REFLECT

When we first met Joseph, he was an egotistical teenager who deliberately irritated his family. Even though he needed to be taught a lesson, this is a pretty tough way to learn: sold into slavery, falsely accused, thrown into prison. How could this be God's plan?

But something happened to Joseph along the way. Maybe the trauma of being rejected by his brothers and trapped far from home prompted some deep reflection. Or maybe he simply realized that his life was headed in the wrong direction. Whatever it was, Joseph had matured. In fact, he had become a model of moral strength (39:8-10) and was sensitive to the opportunities for ministry around him (40:6-8).

How do you react when life is unfair? Do you lash out at the people around you? Do you give up and give in to depression? Do you blame it on God? Joseph had every right to do all of that and more. But he didn't—and there are at least two reasons why.

Joseph put God at the center of his life. When Potiphar's wife tried to tempt him, Joseph knew that God was the One he was accountable to (39:9). And later in prison he gave credit to God for his ability to interpret dreams (40:8). Joseph put God at the center of his life, and it gave him a whole new perspective as well as power to deal with the problems he faced.

Joseph trusted God's plan. On the surface, Joseph's life was a mess. But beneath the surface God was in control (39:2,21). Times of crisis enable us to deepen our relationship with God. We shouldn't go looking for trouble, but tough times do offer us some of the best opportunities to grow in our faith. To seize these opportunities, we must trust that God has a plan, not only when things go well, but even when they don't.

APPLY

What tough times are you experiencing right now? Spend some time in "listening prayer," asking God to show you what he wants to teach you and how you can grow closer to him.

PRAY

Lord, you know I hate it when things go wrong in my life. But I want to grow closer to you, so please help me see what you are doing in the tough places in my life...

Reading 13

THE DEEPER REALITY

PRAY

Lord Jesus, I praise and worship you. I'm overwhelmed by your love for me. Please draw me closer to you today as I read and reflect on your truths…

READ GENESIS 42.

REFLECT

Joseph's brothers weren't thinking about the cruel, unfair thing they had done in the desert years earlier. They were just trying to find some food for the family. But "what goes around comes around," and Joseph realizes it's payback time. Do you think he took some pleasure in accusing his brothers of being spies (42:7-17)?

But this is much more than a story of revenge. When we examine each of the characters, we realize there's something deeper going on. Take Joseph. On the surface he appeared to be extremely successful, powerful, and in control. But inside he carried a wounded soul and was longing for the love and acceptance of his family (42:22-24; see also Genesis 43:30).

The brothers seemed like honest, responsible family men doing their duty in a time of crisis. But inside they were consumed by guilt (42:21) and were afraid that God was about to "zap" them at any moment. Poor old Jacob looked like the wise family patriarch, but inside he had become bitter, afraid, and fatalistic (42:36-38).

Have you ever felt the tension of trying to look good while you feel miserable? We all experience that at some point, and it's one of the worst dilemmas of life. But just looking good will never solve our problems. In fact, looking good makes it more difficult to get help. "How can I admit the way I really feel when people think I'm such a good parent, employee, pastor, Christian? They'll never understand." Therapy can identify our inner problems, but only God through his Holy Spirit can truly resolve them. That's why the church isn't a place for people who think they are perfect. Rather, it's a place where people who aren't afraid to admit they're broken can be healed and set free.

APPLY

What do people think about you? Is that the real you? Are there any issues from your past that you'd like to resolve? Who could you talk to (and pray with) about these things?

PRAY

Heavenly Father, sometimes I exhaust myself just trying to look good. Holy Spirit, please help me find true forgiveness, love, and acceptance in the deepest parts of my life...

Reading 14

MIND GAMES

PRAY

Dear Lord, you know exactly how I'm feeling today as I come to spend time with you. Please open my heart to the things you want me know...

READ GENESIS 43–44.

REFLECT

Joseph had resisted evil in the past (Genesis 39:10), but this temptation was almost too much. After all his brothers had done, it must have been difficult to restrain himself. "Throw me in a pit! Sell me down the river! Wreck my life! Okay, big shots, let's see how *you* like it!" Joseph had the upper hand and the power to crush his helpless siblings. But he didn't, and it's worth asking why.

We don't usually think of anger as a temptation. Actually, it's not anger itself that is so bad. Getting angry is part of being human. Even Jesus got angry (John 2:14-17). But anger can tempt us to respond in the wrong way to those who offend us—"I may be angry, but he deserved it!" That's why the Bible says, "Be angry, and do not sin" (Psalm 4:4; Ephesians 4:26, NKJV).

Joseph bought some time for himself and let the tension build by playing mind games with his brothers. He asked about their father, planted a silver cup in their sacks, and lined them up in birth order. Some may criticize him for not letting them off the hook right away. But real life isn't like that. Some hurts are so deep, it takes time and gradual pressure from God to bring them out in the open. If you're feeling pressure or even anger about things in your past, maybe God is trying to tell you something. One of the best responses to past anger is to pray.

But the main reason Joseph didn't blow his brothers away is that he still loved them. Often we find that underneath our angriest feelings is deep love. That's why lashing out is the worst thing you can do when you're angry. Joseph wisely found a private place to weep (43:30). Honestly grieving about the hurts of the past is another essential step in the healing process. God uses grief to soften our hardened hearts. Eventually, Joseph and his brothers would have to forgive and reconcile. But they weren't there yet. Stay tuned.

APPLY

Are you carrying any hurt from your past? What would you need to do to fully grieve that pain?

PRAY

Heavenly Father, I don't want to hold on to my angry feelings, but I need your help. And Lord, I know I've hurt others by what I've done. Show me how I can help them find healing too…

Reading 15

A CURIOUS WHISPER

PRAY

Heavenly Father, I open my heart and my hands to you in praise. Please accept my worship and open my eyes to whatever I need to see today…

READ GENESIS 45:1–46:7.

REFLECT

Citizen Kane is a classic movie about a powerful and wealthy man named Charles Foster Kane. The film begins with a curious whisper, "Rosebud!" and throughout we wonder what it means. Early in his life Kane's father rejected him, taking the boy's favorite sled and gruffly sending him away. The rest of the movie is the story of how Kane achieved everything in life, except happiness. In the final scene we learn that the name of the favorite sled was…Rosebud. To Charles Kane it symbolized the broken relationship with his father, a fact that haunted him his entire life.

In this passage Joseph reveals not only his identity, but more significantly, the curious whisper that has been driving him all these years: "Is my father still living?" (45:3). That is Joseph's "Rosebud." We may think a broken relationship, especially with someone we've been close to, is no big deal. But it can have a bigger effect than we realize if we don't let God work in us to resolve it.

But let's not forget Joseph's brothers. How did he finally reconcile with them? We've seen Joseph grieving and we've seen him praying. Now we see him forgiving his brothers (45:14-15). Forgiveness is the final step in healing the wounds in our past. It takes time, and we must be open to God's reshaping, but when we forgive, we are miraculously empowered to love again. Forgiveness also opens our eyes to the bigger picture of what God is doing in our lives. As Joseph said, "It was not you who sent me here, but God" (45:8).

Do you want healing from your past hurts? Would you like to be empowered to love again? Are you eager for a clearer understanding of God's will? Then make a commitment, as far as it's possible, to resolve any broken relationships in your life. Unlike Joseph, we may not be able to meet face to face with the person we need to forgive. If the one who's hurt you is no longer living, perhaps you could meet with some other appropriate person and express your willingness to forgive. What a joy it is when the curious whisper is replaced by a song of praise!

APPLY

Is there a "curious whisper" in your mind and heart today about a broken relationship in your life? What initial steps could you take to resolve the problems that are causing that whisper? How will you seek God's help?

PRAY

Lord Jesus, you understand how I feel more than anyone else. Thank you for enduring the Cross so that I could be forgiven… *

---

* Now turn to the Review Journal beginning on page 253 to record your key insights from the last five readings.

Moses and the Exodus

Lights, camera, action…it's time for the story of Moses and the Exodus! Whenever I read this part of the Bible, I think of the classic movie *The Ten Commandments.* I'll never forget the image of Charlton Heston, who played Moses in the film: muscular, handsome, wind blowing through his hair, holding the stone tablets at the top of Mount Sinai.

The life of Moses is one of the most famous and exciting parts of the Bible. Both Christians and Jews look to Moses as an example of spiritual strength and godly conviction. And because of its emphasis on liberation, this saga has given inspiration to oppressed people for centuries—especially those trapped by the evil of slavery. The life of Moses has come to symbolize the human quest for freedom.

But there's more to the life of Moses than what we see in the movies, as you'll discover in these next five readings. For the first forty years of his life, Moses lived among the rich and famous people of Egypt. Then he blew it by losing his temper and spent the next forty years in "nowheresville," living with his in-laws and tending sheep.

Moses would have died in obscurity if it hadn't been for one thing: He had an encounter with God, and that changed everything (Exodus 3:1–4:17). For the last forty years of his life, Moses was a man on a mission—staring down Pharaoh, unleashing the plagues, parting the Red Sea, receiving the Ten Commandments, and leading the Chosen People to the brink of the Promised Land. Talk about a grand finale!

The truth is, God can use us no matter what's happened in our past, no matter how old we are, and no matter how "out of it" we may feel. All it takes is a fresh experience of the living God. After that, you'll never be the same. Haven't seen any burning bushes lately? Don't worry, one of the best ways to encounter God every day is through the Bible and prayer—and that's what you're about to do.

Reading 16

WHAT ARE YOU DOING?

PRAY

Heavenly Father, it is so good just to be still with you. Help me set aside all the distractions in my heart and mind so that I can feel your presence today...

READ EXODUS 1–2.

REFLECT

"You must have been a beautiful baby..." Or at least that's what Pharaoh's daughter seems to have thought about Moses (2:6). Blissfully indifferent to the suffering of the child's family (1:11-14,22), she plucked the baby from the water, and so began the life of one of the Bible's greatest heroes (Matthew 17:1-4).

The name *Moses* sounds like the Hebrew word for *drawn out.* The baby who was drawn out of the river by a princess would draw the Hebrew people out of oppression and slavery many years later. Today our names usually don't have the same level of significance that they did in Bible times, but it's still valuable to consider our origins. What kind of family were you born into? How did your early years shape your character?

The Bible doesn't tell us much about Moses' life after his "lucky break" by the river. All we know is that he became part of the Egyptian elite (2:10). But inside he was an angry young man who finally took matters into his own hands in a futile attempt to save his people (2:12). In God's work, the end doesn't justify the means. That's why prayer is so important in the Christian life; it helps us stay in touch with God's timing and God's ways.

As Moses high-tails it to Midian, he had to wonder, "God, what are you doing?" That's a question we all ask when our lives don't go the way we want them to. You can be sure, God does have a good plan for your life, and he uses every detail—even tough times—to accomplish it. What is God doing in your life right now?

Apply

How have the difficulties in your life prepared you to serve God better? How would you describe your mission in life?

Pray

Dear God, open my eyes to the things you are doing in my life. I want to be all you want me to be, even if that means there are some things I need to change…

Reading 17

ENCOUNTER WITH GOD

PRAY

Heavenly Father, it's good to rest in your presence. Because I know you love me, I'm ready to hear whatever you have to say to me today...

READ EXODUS 3:1–4:17.

REFLECT

At this point in his life, Moses probably wasn't a good example of the power of positive thinking. Eighty years old, plodding away in a dead-end job, living with his in-laws. No wonder he wanted to be by himself (3:1).

God often chooses people the world overlooks (1 Samuel 16:7). David was an unimpressive shepherd boy; Mary was an unknown Jewish girl; Peter was a scaly fisherman; and Moses was a burned-out retiree with no pension! It's worth reflecting on the "forgotten people" around you. If we assume that God works only through "Christian leaders," we may miss some of the most powerful things God wants to do. The exciting thing about the Christian life is that God can break in when you least expect it.

What is it like to have an encounter with God? Many people over the centuries have tried to find God in all sorts of ways. That desire is certainly good, but as Moses discovered, God is already there. He's present everywhere, and he's waiting for us (Psalm 46:10). The real question is, do we really want to meet him...and on his terms?

Notice the progression in Moses' interaction with God. It starts with curiosity (3:3), then moves to fear (3:6), and finally to outright rejection (4:13). When Moses realized God's plan for him would be difficult, he questioned if he wanted the job. If you are really searching, God doesn't mind honest doubts and questions. But when they become a smoke screen for rejecting God, that's another matter (4:13-14).

But the most amazing thing is that God sees what we are going through (3:7), and he promises to be with us (3:12). The God of the universe wants you to know who he is and what he is like. And he's gone to the most extraordinary lengths to help you understand that.

Apply

When and in what ways have you encountered God in your life? How have those encounters changed you?

Pray

God, I admit that sometimes I am hesitant to come into your presence. But I really want to know more of you. Please open my mind, heart, and will to what you want to do in me today...

Reading 18

A PLAGUE OF DOUBT

PRAY

Lord God, you are worthy of all my praise. I begin this time in your word by worshiping you…

READ EXODUS 6:28–11:10.

REFLECT

Here we have one of the classic battles between good and evil in the Bible—for that matter, in all of human history. Ten times Moses confronted Pharaoh with a plague and a message from God, "Let my people go" (7:16). But Pharaoh's incredible stubbornness proved to be his undoing. Flat-out rejecting God isn't the only way our hearts can become hardened. It can simply be the result of gradually doing things our own way. But in the end the result is the same: a broken relationship with God.

Why did God bother with the ten plagues? After all, he could have saved the ecosystem and gone straight to number ten. Or he could have caused Pharaoh to keel over and given power to a more tolerant successor. The answer has two parts. The first part is very broad: God wanted to proclaim his name, to let people know that he is the Lord (9:16; 10:2). He wants everybody in the whole world for all time to know that he is God, that he is powerful, and that he is worthy of our worship. We learn this from the Bible and also see it in creation (Psalm 19:1-4; Romans 1:20).

The second part of the answer is very personal: God also works in the lives of individuals, shaping and preparing them for the work he has called them to do. Consider Moses. He wasted the best years of his life, and when God tried to give him a second chance, he resisted and rejected God's plan. Moses needed one of those buttons for his robe—"Be patient. God isn't finished with me yet." The ten plagues were not just for Pharaoh. It seems that Moses, too, needed to be convinced that God alone was the Lord.

If you want to know God, the starting place is believing that he is the Lord over the entire world. But to *really* know him, you must make him the Lord of *your* life as well. That's what being a follower of Jesus is all about.

APPLY

What did it take (or will it take) to convince you that God is Lord over the whole world? over your own life?

PRAY

Lord Jesus, thank you for the incredible lengths you went to in order to have a relationship with me. Help me to be your willing and faithful follower today...

Reading 19

SPARE ME!

PRAY

Lord Jesus, you are the Way, the Truth, and the Life (John 14:6). Please help me draw closer to you and my heavenly Father as I read and reflect on your Word...

READ EXODUS 12:1-42.

REFLECT

Have you ever wondered what Passover is all about? Most calendars include it, and Jewish people all over the world still celebrate it. But as you read these verses, you have to wonder what God was thinking. Why the elaborate instructions about the lamb and sharing, how fast to eat the meal, and what to do with the blood (12:1-11)? Our passage gives us two big hints.

God's first purpose for the Passover was judgment (12:12). Not only were the Egyptians cruelly forcing the Jews to be their slaves, they were also deeply involved in idolatry. God can't stand it when we oppress others or worship anything or anyone other than him. The Egyptians were doing both, and God had to stop it with a very severe punishment (12:29-30). Today we may not oppress people with a whip; it may be economic or social oppression. Our idolatry may not involve carved statues; it may be as simple as caring too much about how we look or how our favorite sports team is doing. The point is, we are on dangerous ground when we hold people down or let someone or something become more important to us than God.

God's second purpose for the Passover was to create a reminder (12:14). He wanted his people to remember how he set them free from oppression. But there was more to it than that. The lamb and the blood were symbols of a much greater salvation to come. Jesus was "the Lamb of God" who shed his own blood to take away the sins of the world (John 1:29). In fact, Jesus specifically applied all the imagery of the Passover to himself (Matthew 26:26-30). This was God's strategy for saving humankind from sin.

And what about poor old Pharaoh? After ten horrible plagues and the loss of his own son, he finally gave in (12:31). How ironic that Pharaoh asked for a parting blessing from Moses and Aaron (12:32). Pharaoh thought he could resist God or manipulate things to go his way. But as this passage shows us, God is in charge and he is at work accomplishing his purposes in the world. The best response we can give is to do what the Israelites did: obey God immediately (12:28).

APPLY

Is there anything in your life that has a stronger hold on you than God? What would it take to put God at the center of your life? How would it change your priorities and actions?

PRAY

Lord God, I know you are the One in charge of this world and of my life. Please set me free from everything that holds me back from worshiping you with my whole heart...

Reading 20

THE DEFINING MOMENT

PRAY

"Your word is a lamp to my feet and a light for my path" (Psalm 119:105). May that be so today, dear Lord...

READ EXODUS 13:17–14:31.

REFLECT

Some people think that parting the Red Sea was the defining moment for Moses. It certainly must have been spectacular to see all that water piling up in a great wall. And who's going to challenge a leader who can do something like that? "Whatever you say, Chief."

But our passage reveals a more significant defining moment for Moses, and it comes just prior to parting the sea. Imagine how Moses felt. He was pinned against the water. The most powerful army in the world was bearing down on him with a score to settle, and his own people were on the verge of mutiny (14:11-12). Moses had to feel as though he'd made a big mistake that was going to cause a huge disaster.

Have you ever felt that way when you've tried to do something for God? Perhaps you've taken a leadership position in the church or in a ministry, and the whole thing fell apart, with everyone blaming you. Some people get bitter or give up. But disasters, though painful, present us with the best opportunities to grow; they force our faith to a higher level.

Instead of rationalizing or running, Moses stood up and boldly proclaimed his trust in God (14:13-14). This is one of the best examples of Christian leadership in the entire Bible. What God had been teaching Moses through the progression of plagues—that he is powerful and has a plan, and that he wants us to trust and obey him—he now put into action. It's one thing to know all the right answers; it's another to publicly take action when the pressure is on. But when we do that, we have a defining moment in our own relationship with God.

Apply

What have been the defining moments in your relationship with God? Have any of them involved pressure or even disaster? Is there a situation in your life right now in which you could trust God with more boldness? What would it look like to trust God more in that area?

Pray

Heavenly Father, you know I'd rather avoid problems. Help me know whether the pressures I face are the result of my bad judgment or your desire to stretch my faith in you... *

---

* Now turn to the Review Journal beginning on page 253 to record your key insights from the last five readings.

The Law and the Land

After the Israelites broke free of their bondage in Egypt, their main objective was to find a home. Land has always been important to the Jewish people, not only because they've wanted a place to call their own but also because God had promised it to them. It is that quest to reach the Promised Land that animates our next five readings.

Sometimes people say, "The journey is more important than the destination." Perhaps there's a bit of truth in that for the children of Israel, because God did some incredible things while they wandered in the desert. We've already seen how he parted the Red Sea and destroyed the Egyptian army. Now we'll see God thundering on Mount Sinai as he gives Moses the Ten Commandments. He'll also part the Jordan River and give the Israelites a tremendous military victory at Jericho. As they enter the Promised Land, the Israelites will have momentum on their side.

There's an important theme running through these readings that you'll want to be aware of. Any success Israel had was due not to their large army, effective strategies, or good luck, but it was the result of their willingness to listen to and obey God. Simple as that. It took Moses many years to learn that lesson, but once he finally got it, God really used him. Joshua had the advantage of watching Moses, so he learned the lesson faster. But you'll see that cultivating a willingness and ability to hear the Word of God and put it into action is the key to growth and effectiveness in the Christian life.

Our readings do give us a hint of dark clouds on the horizon for the

Chosen People. The golden calf was Israel's first direct experience with idolatry. For the rest of the Old Testament, they struggled with this destructive tendency. In the end it alienated them from God and brought a terrible punishment. But it also highlighted their need for a Messiah, a Savior, and that's what the New Testament is all about.

Reading 21

TOP TEN LIST

PRAY

Thank you, Lord God, that you have made it clear in your Word how you want me to live. Help me read and understand with my heart today…

READ EXODUS 19:1–20:21.

REFLECT

People like to argue about the Ten Commandments. Should they be posted in courthouses and public schools? Do they have historical or religious significance? It's an argument that makes good folks go ballistic.

But in all the hoo-ha, most people miss the most important point. The Ten Commandments are not just a list of "Thou shalts" and "Thou shalt nots." That's the kind of religion many people want. But God isn't trying to start a religion; he's trying to build a relationship with his people (19:4-6). That's what makes these famous commandments so important; they show us what God really cares about. And if we want to relate to him, we must care about these things too.

It may help to divide the commandments into three groups. The first group centers on *our relationship with God* (20:2-11). There's only one God (20:3), and he warns us to accept no substitutes (20:4-6). We mustn't be too casual—or worse—in referring to him (20:7). And we must regularly honor and worship him (20:8-11). Since he is the Sovereign Creator of all things, can we do any less?

The next group addresses *our relationship with others* (20:12-14,16). Before we can "love everybody," we need to start with those closest to us: our parents (20:12) and spouses (20:14). The patterns we develop here will affect all our other relationships. Our next challenge is to be truthful with our neighbors (20:16)—easier said than done in a world of manipulation and compromise. That's why it's a relief to have at least one easy commandment (20:13). The problem is, Jesus didn't think it was so easy (Matthew 5:21-22).

The third group deals with *our relationship to things* (20:15,17). A willingness to steal (20:15) begins when we aren't content with what we have (20:17). The desire for more is a strong motivator that can pull us away from God (1 Timothy 6:6-10). If more people had a right relationship with God, others, and things, the world really would be a different place. No wonder people would rather argue about the Ten Commandments than simply obey them.

APPLY

What are the things that improve or erode your relationship with God? Which commandments do you feel God might be calling you to work on this week?

PRAY

Lord in heaven, I really want to know you better. Please help me care about the things that are important to you. And thank you for loving and forgiving me when I fail...

Reading 22

UP CLOSE AND PERSONAL

PRAY

"Search me, O God, and know my heart; test me and know my anxious thoughts. See if there is any offensive way in me, and lead me in the way everlasting" (Psalm 139:23-24).

READ EXODUS 32–34.

REFLECT

In this passage Aaron delivered one of the funniest lines in the Bible (32:24)—"I threw [the gold] into the fire, and out came this calf!" Talk about lame excuses! Put him in charge for just a few days, and he let the people run wild.

But before we laugh too hard at Aaron, we need to look at ourselves. With all we know about God, and after all he's done for us, how quickly we turn our backs on him to binge on sin. Even the apostle Paul struggled with this tendency (Romans 7:15-20). Being a Christian doesn't exempt us from temptation and sin. But through Jesus, God has given us the only way to break its power over our lives (1 John 1:9).

This passage also gives us a glimpse of God's angry side (32:9-10). He hates sin, a reality we shouldn't take lightly. Moses hated sin too (32:19-20). At first it may seem as if he overreacted (32:25-28), but there can be no compromise with sin. The pursuit of holiness sometimes requires drastic changes. But Moses did more than get angry; he was willing to stand in the gap to do whatever it took to save his people (32:11-14,31-32). His action provides us with a hint of what Jesus would do many years later.

But perhaps the most amazing part of this passage is the interaction between God and Moses. They developed a very personal relationship (33:11). That's what God really wants with all of us. He has no interest in a world of religious zombies. He created men and women in his own image, and he wants them to acknowledge that he is Lord by loving and following him with their whole hearts. He even sent his own Son, Jesus Christ, to die on the cross to make that possible.

APPLY

How would you describe your relationship with God at this time? What things pull you away from him? What things draw you closer?

PRAY

O God, we both know how quickly I give in to sin. Please forgive me, for Jesus' sake, and help me to draw closer to you today...

Reading 23

LEARN IT AND LIVE IT

PRAY

Dear Lord, I'm so thankful that you've given me your Word. As I meditate on it today, guide my heart to the message you want me to hear and apply…

READ JOSHUA 1.

REFLECT

New pastors often struggle when they have to follow in the footsteps of a beloved longtime pastor. People can't help comparing the new leader to the old one, usually unfavorably. It can be a difficult time for both the new pastor and the congregation. So imagine how Joshua felt at this point in his "career." How could he top Moses?

But a quick look back reveals that God had been preparing Joshua for this leadership challenge. Joshua had witnessed Moses leading the Israelites, and he had seen Moses develop a real relationship with God (Exodus 32:17; 33:11). One of the best ways to grow in our spiritual lives is to find a mentor—someone older and wiser in the faith. If you want to learn it, watch someone who's living it. If you've been a Christian for a long time, pray that God will lead you to those he wants you to coach on his behalf. It's an important ministry.

After Moses, God made a special effort to encourage Joshua for the task ahead. He promised to give him land, success, and a leadership platform like the one he gave Moses (1:3-6). Best of all, God promised to be with Joshua (1:5). Someday you may be called to serve God in a difficult situation, one that stretches you beyond your abilities. But if God has called you to a task, he will be with you. That means difficult situations can be opportunities to experience God.

In return for all God's promises and help, he only asked that Joshua obey him (1:7). It sounds so easy, but it's not, mostly because we are sinful. That's why God gave Joshua his Word and instructed him to really soak it up (1:8). If you want to live an effective Christian life, the secret is reflecting (meditating) on God's Word and applying (doing) what it says. That's why right now is the most important part of your day.

APPLY

Which challenge fits you best at this time: finding a spiritual mentor or serving as a spiritual mentor? Or maybe both? Explain. How will you go about doing this?

PRAY

Heavenly Father, thank you for the people who have influenced me to follow you. Please help me to keep growing and show me how I can help others grow too…

Reading 24

EFFECTIVE CHRISTIAN LEADERSHIP

PRAY

"Oh, how I love your law! I meditate on it all day long" (Psalm 119:97). Lord, I come to this time open to finding a particular truth that I can think about today...

READ JOSHUA 3–4.

REFLECT

When Joshua led the people through the Jordan River, it was an exact replay of the time Moses led the people through the Red Sea, only this time Israel's enemies had learned not to give chase! God was using the similarities between the two events to strengthen Joshua's leadership position (3:7).

But Joshua's success was the result of much more than his past association with a spiritual celebrity. He had cultivated the habit of listening to God and obeying right away (Joshua 1:7,9-13). That's the key to effective Christian leadership: following orders from God. In addition, Joshua had two other traits that made him effective in God's work. The first was bold faith; he publicly announced his belief in God's power (Joshua 1:11). The second was humility. Even though he knew God had decided to honor him with acclaim, he didn't let it go to his head. No matter what God asks you to do, these are the traits that will make you successful.

Our passage also presents us with some interesting symbols. The ark of the covenant symbolizes God's presence among the people of Israel. The Jordan River symbolizes the death experience for many—the end of the journey and the beginning of the Promised Land. And the stones from the middle of the river were to be a sign of what God had done on behalf of his people.

What are the symbols in your Christian life? You may want to think about, maybe even write about the significant times in your relationship with God. Is there a symbol you could use to remind yourself of the lesson God taught you? But be careful not to focus so much on the symbol that you forget its meaning. Entering the Promised Land was a spiritual high point and an important symbol for Israel. Unfortunately, over time they forgot the One who got them there.

Apply

Which is the bigger need in your life right now: a greater knowledge of God's Word or a greater passion for God? What can you do to begin meeting that need?

Pray

Lord Jesus, thank you for the times in my life when you've met me in a new way. Keep me hungry for your Word and passionate to know you better…

Reading 25

I DID IT MY WAY?

PRAY

Lord, I praise you for being such an awesome and loving God. I want to take time right now to thank you for your many blessings in my life…

READ JOSHUA 5:13–6:27.

REFLECT

If you've ever been to Sunday school, you've heard the story about how the walls of Jericho came a-tumbling down. Crash! God wanted the Promised Land free of all those who worshiped idols and free of the detestable practices that went with them. The sad part was that although the Israelites got off to this spectacular start, they never finished the job. And it proved to be their undoing.

But this passage raises an uncomfortable question: Wasn't God a little extreme? Wouldn't it have been better for him to let everyone worship in his or her own way? The hard fact is, God is the Creator and Lord of all. That's the message he was communicating throughout Israel's history. To set our own conditions on God is not worship; it's rejection. The clay doesn't tell the potter what to make (Isaiah 45:9).

That doesn't mean God is intolerant. Consider what happened to Rahab. She was a non-Jew and a prostitute living in a city marked for destruction. The Bible doesn't condone her sin. But it does show that those who turn to

God and demonstrate it by their actions will be saved (Joshua 2:1-21). That's not intolerance; that's God's all-embracing love and free gift of forgiveness. Those who insist on going their own way run the risk of forfeiting that gift.

Imagine how you would have felt marching around the city of Jericho. No doubt the Israelites had to endure some "trash-talk" from the guards on the wall. But God's ways are not our ways, and once again we are reminded of the need to listen to and obey God. That's a lesson God really wants to teach us, because it's the key to growth and effectiveness in the Christian life.

APPLY

Has your faith in God ever caused you to do something that seemed odd? What happened? Do you sense God calling you to take a step of faith in some way this week? Explain.

PRAY

Heavenly Father, I don't claim to understand everything about you, but I do believe you are the Lord, and I want to follow You. Please help me hear and obey what you want to say to me… *

---

* Now turn to the Review Journal beginning on page 253 to record your key insights from the last five readings.

THE JUDGES

The book of Judges is one of those parts of the Old Testament that is often overlooked. Genesis and Exodus were new and exciting. The miracle of Creation was followed by the adventures of Abraham, Isaac, Jacob, Joseph, Moses, and Joshua. And just ahead are the books of 1 and 2 Samuel and 1 and 2 Kings, where we meet two of Israel's greatest kings, David and Solomon. After that we dive into the two most popular books in the entire Bible, Psalms and Proverbs.

But hold on, we missed something. What happened to God's people between the time of the patriarchs and the time of the kings? That's what the book of Judges is all about. The people of Israel had finally put down roots in the Promised Land, and there they began to grow and expand into a great nation. The problem, at least from their point of view, was that they didn't have a king.

The problem from God's point of view was that they kept turning away from him to worship idols. Why would they want to worship the Canaanite fertility gods—Baal and the Ashtoreths—instead of the one true God who had brought them out of Egypt with so many demonstrations of his love and power? For that matter, why do people turn their backs on God today? That's one of the underlying questions for us to ponder in these next five readings.

Because of the people's idolatry, God punished them by allowing the surrounding nations—the Midianites and the Philistines—to attack and oppress them for long periods of time. You can almost hear God saying, "How many times do we have to go through this before you learn?" But even so, when the people finally came to their senses and cried out to God, he raised up special leaders called judges to save Israel from the consequences of their sin. The sad part is, after a few years they forgot God again and started the process all over.

The book of Judges isn't all gloom and doom, though. It contains the stories of some of the most intriguing Bible characters—Deborah, Gideon, and Samson. And our readings finish with one of the most romantic stories in the Bible, the book of Ruth.

Sometimes the parts of the Bible that are least familiar to us give us the greatest insights. That's because we don't have as many preconceptions about them; we are able to take a fresh look at what God is saying. That's a good way to read any Bible passage.

Reading 26

ENDANGERED SPECIES

PRAY

Heavenly Father, my desire is to hear your voice. Please open the ears of my heart so that I may truly listen to what you have to say to me…

READ JUDGES 2:6–3:6.

REFLECT

Have you ever heard someone say, "Christianity is one generation away from becoming extinct," as if the postmodern worldview is about to make God irrelevant? That can be an unnerving thought. But, in fact, Christianity is *always* one generation away from extinction. Unless Jesus' followers communicate the reality of the gospel and the truth of God's Word, the next generation will never know.

We certainly see an example of this in today's reading. Joshua and the leaders around him had died, and they took the stories of God's great work with them to the grave (2:7). No matter how old you are, you have an important mission for the rest of your life: Tell others, especially younger people, what God has done for you.

Unfortunately, the Israelites failed to do that, and it brought about a depressing cycle in their history (2:10-19). They turned away from God, worshiped idols, and experienced disaster. Then in desperation they cried out to

God. He raised up judges to lead them—and saved them. But before too long, the cycle began again…and again…and again.

Have you ever experienced that cycle in your life? Turning our backs on God or just gradually taking little steps away from him can lead to some painful consequences. But even then, God is at work. Note that he intended to use the disasters to test his people (2:22), to find out if they really would turn to him when the chips were down. If there's anything good about falling away from God, it's that our relationship with him is much stronger after we return (James 1:2-4).

APPLY

Where are you in your relationship with God? Are you close to him? gradually falling away? experiencing disaster? What have you learned from the tests God has allowed you to go through?

PRAY

Lord God, I'm grateful that even when I falter, your desire is to help me grow closer to you. Show me how I can encourage at least one younger person in his or her relationship with you…

Reading 27

GIRL POWER

PRAY

Holy Spirit, I invite you to be present with me during this time. Please give me a sharp mind and a tender heart as I look into your Word today…

READ JUDGES 4–5.

REFLECT

If you're looking for a Bible passage that will make women and girls feel powerful, this is it. The only female judge in the Bible, Deborah broke the glass ceiling in Israel. And the hero of this story is Jael, a young woman who had the smarts and the guts to take out the military commander, Sisera. You go, girl!

But to really hear what this passage has to say, we must look deeper than the "boys against the girls" theme. First, notice the source of Deborah's leadership. She didn't try to take charge, and she wasn't interested in being up at the front lines (4:9-10). She simply said and did what God had told her (4:6-7,14), and it had a powerful effect.

As we saw in the life of Joshua, a spiritual leader is one who follows orders from God. If that's true, the path to Christian leadership is not just to attain a prominent position or to be over a big staff. It's about developing the ability to listen to God. And whether you are a man or a woman, a boy or a girl, you can be that kind of leader (Joel 2:28-29). In fact, the church is desperate for people who know how to hear and follow God's direction.

A second theme in this passage has to do with courage, another quality that isn't limited by gender. No one could have imagined what "the little homemaker" had in mind when Jael invited Sisera into her tent (4:17-21). She didn't learn *that* at the ladies' auxiliary. But God used Jael's bold act to defeat the powerful Canaanites. The point is, we can't limit God from using whomever he wants to do his work. In the end, it's our ability to listen to God and our willingness to rely on his power that make the difference.

Apply

How could you cultivate the ability to hear and follow God's direction more? In what area of your life do you most need to rely on God's power?

Pray

Heavenly Father, open my eyes to see all the people you want to use to do your work. And with your help, I intend to be one of them...

Reading 28

HOW CAN I BE SURE?

PRAY

"I wait for the LORD, my soul waits, and in his word I put my hope. My soul waits for the Lord more than watchmen wait for the morning, more than watchmen wait for the morning" (Psalm 130:5-6).

READ JUDGES 6–7.

REFLECT

The very first word in this passage tells us everything we need to know about the spiritual state of Israel: "Again..." (6:1). How many disasters will it take for the Chosen People to learn to obey God? Aaron had no idea what his compromise in the desert would lead to (Exodus 32:1-6). But that's how sin works; it doesn't seem like a big deal at first, but left unchecked, it grows and eventually destroys us and others. The only way to stop it is to repent, and the sooner the better.

Enter Gideon, a man not really interested in being a leader (6:11-15). But God saw his potential (6:12) and used this difficult time in Israel's history to prepare him for a bigger challenge ahead. That should be an encouragement if you're in a frustrating situation right now. Perhaps God is preparing you for your next assignment on his behalf. What do you need to learn now?

Some question whether Gideon's request for signs reveals a lack of faith

(6:17-40). Can we ask for a sign today? Not if we make it some kind of formula, a gimmick to get an "answer." But if we genuinely seek God in faith, we can ask him to make his will clear to us. Real power and conviction come when we prayerfully wait for confirmation from God. That's what happened with Gideon.

But Gideon's success was the result of two other things: He was empowered by the Spirit (6:34), and he was forced to rely on God's power (7:2). That was the whole point of reducing the army from thirty-two thousand men to three hundred men. Don't be discouraged if you feel you don't have enough resources to do God's work. All he needs is one person who's willing to listen and obey.

APPLY

How do you listen to God? What is one particular need or issue for which you need to prayerfully wait on God for confirmation?

PRAY

Sovereign Lord, it's so encouraging to read about what you can do through those who trust and obey you. Please show me how to let more of your power work through me...

Reading 29

LADIES' MAN

PRAY

Lord, I want to prepare myself to meet you today in a time of confession. Please show me the things that are blocking my relationship with you…

READ JUDGES 13–16.

REFLECT

What in the world happened between chapters 13 and 14? Manoah and his wife (we never learn her name) seem like the model of godly parenting (13:8,12). They knew their miracle child had been specially chosen and empowered by God for a great work in Israel (13:5,25). But somehow, Samson developed a fatal character flaw; he had no self-control, and it proved to be his undoing.

Christian parents who have wayward children need special support and prayer. It can be incredibly painful to watch the ones we love make destructive choices. But we can find encouragement in knowing that sometimes God is at work in ways that aren't so obvious (14:4).

Samson's lack of self-control expressed itself in two ways: lust and anger. His thoughtless pursuit of women seems comical, but it produced a string of broken relationships and violence. Not funny. If God has called you to married life, finding a spouse who shares your commitment to Christ and having the determination to work through the ups and downs of a lifelong relationship will be hard work. But it's the only way to find the love and satisfaction Samson never found.

In the end, Samson became the classic example of a talented but flawed leader. Maybe Delilah's performance fooled him, or maybe he just gave up. But the real tragedy of Samson's life is that deep down he knew he had been running from God all along (16:17). The greatest victory in Samson's life was not his temple-crashing defeat of the Philistines. It was the fact that, in his brokenness, he finally turned back to God (16:28).

APPLY

What are the motivating factors in your relationships with those of the opposite sex? What steps could you take to develop relationships that honor God (1 Timothy 5:1-2)?

PRAY

Lord God, I thank you for the people who are closest to me in life. Enable me to be a godly example and encouragement to them this week....

Reading 30

LOVE STORY

PRAY

Lord Jesus, you gave up everything to die on the cross for my sin. I don't understand why you love me so much, but I am very, very grateful...

READ RUTH 1–4.

REFLECT

What a great love story. There's tragedy, intrigue, romance, and even a happy ending. The story of Ruth is a bright spot in the depressing sin cycle we've seen in the book of Judges. But this is much more than a romance novel. Ruth is a tremendous example of godly character (3:11), and that's what makes this short book so helpful to us today.

Ruth's life got off to a traditional start. For ten years she was married and surrounded by her extended family (1:4-5). But when both her husband and her father-in-law died, Ruth's world fell apart. Tough times often reveal our true character. We can become resentful like Naomi (1:20-21). Or we can let God use the detours in our lives to make us stronger and more like him. No matter what happens, that's the choice we must make.

So what did the tough times reveal about Ruth's character?

- She was *loyal;* she didn't abandon her family even though it was in her best interest to do so (1:14).

- She was *optimistic;* she wasn't bitter like her mother-in-law (2:2).
- She was a *hard worker;* she didn't give up on life because something bad had happened to her (2:7).
- She was *submissive;* she worked within the customs of her day (3:5-6).
- She had *integrity;* she didn't resort to sinful shortcuts in building a relationship with her future husband (3:7-14).
- And finally, she had *faith;* she committed her life to God no matter where that would take her (1:16).

Today many people try to achieve success by having a lot of things, by knowing the right people, or even by just looking the part. But Ruth's way was to cultivate a noble character and then trust God to bless her as he saw fit. And he certainly did. God gave Ruth a happy marriage to a prominent man, wealth and security, and best of all, a son who became the grandfather of King David and an ancestor of Jesus Christ (Matthew 1:5-6). Not bad for a former homeless widow.

APPLY

What tough times are you facing right now? What do you think God might want to reveal about the character he's given you?

PRAY

Heavenly Father, I need your help to face the problems in my life. Most of all, I need you to help me become the person you want me to be… *

---

* Now turn to the Review Journal beginning on page 253 to record your key insights from the last five readings.

The Rise of Israel

Who would lead the people of Israel now that they had settled in the Promised Land? That's the big question being worked out in our next five readings. As we've seen, God's plan was to form Abraham's descendants into a "great nation" and through them to bring "great blessing" to all people (Genesis 12:2-3). That blessing would be a Savior for the sins of the entire world—Jesus Christ.

Because of their unique place in his plan, the Israelites experienced God's direct help and guidance over the years. It was God who freed the children of Israel from captivity in Egypt; it was God who led them through the desert with pillars of cloud and fire; it was God who brought them to the Promised Land. And along the way it was God who took the initiative to reveal his priorities by giving them the Law at Mount Sinai. Since the very beginning, God had been powerfully and miraculously leading his people.

But, as we will see, the Israelites became uncomfortable with God's "leadership style." He absolutely refused to let them worship other gods or participate in all the things that went with it. So instead, they wanted a king "like all the other nations" (1 Samuel 8:19-20). On the surface this didn't seem like such an outrageous request. But behind Israel's desire for a king was a rejection of God's rule over them (1 Samuel 8:6-7). We must make the same decision today: either to follow Jesus and be part of God's kingdom or to go our own way. It's a decision that has eternal consequences.

In spite of the people's subtle rejection, God didn't abandon them. He gave them the kings they wanted, and he continued working out his plan through these rulers. As a result, we are introduced to some of the Bible's greatest characters. We meet Samuel, the boy who listened to God; Saul,

Israel's talented first king, who came to a tragic end; and David, Israel's greatest king and a man after God's own heart.

Our readings bring us to the pinnacle of Israel's history, the one time when they had both the land and peace. As we know from reading the rest of the Bible and our daily newspapers, it didn't last. But what a glorious time it was.

Reading 31

THE REAL WORLD

PRAY

Dear Lord, I know I'm not perfect, but I'm committed to becoming the person you want me to be. I'm open to whatever you want to say to me from your Word today...

READ 1 SAMUEL 1–3.

REFLECT

One of the things that gives the Bible the ring of truth is that it records the real stories of real people. Although the events in this reading took place thousands of years ago, they seem as if they could be happening today. Let's take a closer look and see what lessons we can apply to our lives now.

The stressed-out wife. As we've seen in earlier readings—Genesis 16:1-10; 18:11-12—the inability to have children was a source of shame in ancient Israel. For Hannah, it was the cause of deep stress and personal trauma (1:8,15). In spite of her pain, Hannah candidly poured out her heart to God and asked for his help (1:10-17). That's what real prayer is all about.

The overly tolerant father. For all his good qualities, Eli failed to discipline his sons when they were young, and soon they were out of control (2:12-17,22-25). Today many parents think the loving thing to do is let teenagers make their own decisions. But setting appropriate limits for our children is one of the most important responsibilities of parents. That's real love.

The faithful child. Several times in this reading, we see a contrast between Samuel and Eli's sons, Hophni and Phinehas. What was the key difference? Samuel was willing to listen to God (3:10), while the older boys were not (2:17). The most important lesson any child (or adult) has to learn is how to listen to and follow God wholeheartedly. That's the ultimate reality check.

APPLY

Which character from our reading do you most identify with? What do you learn from his or her experience that can help you? How could you do a better job of modeling your commitment to Christ to those around you—especially young people?

PRAY

Heavenly Father, I really do love you, but I need your help to demonstrate that to others. Please help me become an effective witness for you…

Reading 32

HAIL TO THE CHIEF

PRAY

Dear Lord, thank you for the freedom I have to read the Bible. Now I ask for the gift of your presence as I listen to what you want to say to me today…

READ 1 SAMUEL 8–10.

REFLECT

It doesn't seem like such a big deal that a developing nation would want its own king. After all, who's going to run the government, spend tax dollars, or be the commander in chief (8:10-18)? Somebody's got to be the boss.

But underneath Israel's "reasonable" desire for a king was a rebellious motivation; they wanted to be like everyone else (8:20). After all that God had done for Israel, they still wanted to go their own way (8:6-9). That's a temptation every Christian faces. If we aren't careful, the pressure to conform, to fit in, to be accepted, can gradually lead us away from God. Jesus simply said, "Follow me" (Mark 1:16-18). It sounds easy, but what he is really asking is to be the King of our lives. That's what it means to say, "Jesus is Lord."

Even so, Saul seemed like a good choice for Israel's "first" king. He was tall, impressive, humble, and even religious. Sometimes God gives us what we ask for, even though it's not his first choice for us. It may lead us down a road of greater difficulty, as it did for the Israelites. But God loves us so much that he's willing to use even the detours we take to teach us some important lessons.

In Saul's case, God was also willing to give him the most important trait of an effective Christian leader—a heart open to the leading of the Spirit (10:5-10). That's a trait worth cultivating whether you are a leader or not, because it's how God can use you to make a difference in the lives of the people around you. Notice that being led by the Spirit is a two-sided coin—God works in our hearts, but we must develop the ability to hear him. We can do that by reading the Bible, praying, and using our gifts for the benefit of other Christians (1 Corinthians 12). Those are the disciplines that enable us to hear and obey our King today.

Apply

When you say, "Jesus is Lord," what do you mean? What can you do this week to cultivate the ability to hear God better?

Pray

Lord Jesus, I want to be a fully committed follower of yours. Please help me prepare my heart so that you can use me to do your will...

Reading 33

ONLY A BOY NAMED DAVID

PRAY

Heavenly Father, open my eyes to see something new about you today. Open my heart to your love and presence as I seek you…

READ 1 SAMUEL 16:1–18:16.

REFLECT

Our passage today contains a Bible story that has become part of our popular culture. When a lone citizen challenges city hall, when a start-up business competes with a large corporation, when an underdog team plays the world champions…why, it's like David taking on Goliath. But what really was the key to David's success?

First of all, it took guts for a teenager to volunteer to fight such a huge warrior (17:32). No doubt David's brothers thought his victory was due to a lucky shot. But the real reason David killed Goliath had little to do with guts or luck. It was God's doing.

Notice that God had chosen David (16:12), filled him with his Spirit (16:13), and stayed with him all the way (18:14). God expects us to use the talents and abilities he has given us to do his work, but we must remember that the final results depend on him. That's why success and humility must go hand-in-hand. Ultimately, David won because he understood Goliath was picking a fight with God (17:45).

That's not to say David was perfect. Grouchy old Eliab thought David was conceited and wicked (17:28). Perhaps he was at times; there's often a grain of truth in every criticism. But the Bible makes clear that David had developed an instinct for depending on God in other stressful situations (17:34-37), so when the pressure was on with Goliath, he was ready.

David's greatest strength was his heart for God (Acts 13:22). It's natural to be attracted to people who have all the right stuff—beauty, intelligence, athletic ability, charm, fame, wealth...whatever. But God makes it clear he's looking for something deeper than that (16:7). He's looking for people with hearts that are totally committed to him. That's what matters most.

APPLY

How have you reacted to your successes in life? Who around you has a heart for God? How can you tell? What can you do to cultivate a heart for God?

PRAY

Lord God, forgive me for comparing myself to others on superficial things. Please help me develop a heart that is eager to know and follow your will...

Reading 34

FIRST IMPULSE

PRAY

God in heaven, how wonderful it is to be alone with you. I want to set aside all the distractions in my mind and heart so that I can focus only on what you want to say to me today…

READ 1 SAMUEL 23:7–24:22.

REFLECT

For me, Saul is one of the most tragic figures in the Bible. He started out so well. He was talented, humble, chosen by God, and filled with the Spirit. He seemed like a sure success for God. But in today's reading Saul has become jealous, paranoid, and sinful. Worst of all, he knew his days were numbered (23:17). What happened?

For all his positive traits, Saul had one fatal flaw: an impulse for doing things his own way instead of God's (1 Samuel 13:1-15; 15:10). That's a good description of sin. Over time that impulse warped his relationships (23:21-23), ruined his judgment (1 Samuel 28:1-25), and caused his destruction (1 Samuel 31:1-6). Is your first impulse in every situation to obey God? It's worth spending some time in prayerful reflection on that point so you'll be ready when you face temptation or testing.

But we shouldn't conclude that there was no hope for Saul. Imagine how different things would have been if he had repented and recommitted himself to obeying God. No matter what we've done, no matter how much we've disobeyed God, he is always willing to give us a fresh start (1 John 1:9). That's the essence of the Good News.

In contrast to Saul, David's first impulse was to trust God in every situation of his life. Even when he had every right to kill Saul in self-defense, David held back, preferring to let God do things his way (24:12). Have you been unfairly treated, betrayed, or wronged by someone close to you? It rarely helps to lash out and give them a taste of their own medicine. It's far better to pray, "Lord, this is not fair, and I'm angry about it, but I'm determined to make choices that please you." You'll be amazed at how God can use that kind of honest trust in him to change even the most difficult situation (24:16-21).

APPLY

Think of some situations when you've been tempted. What was your first impulse? Think of one situation in which you need to courageously trust God. What will that require of you?

PRAY

Lord God, I want my first impulse to be a willingness to obey you. I know I can't do that in my own strength, so I ask you to fill me with your Spirit now and always...

Reading 35

ATTABOY, DAVID!

PRAY

Heavenly Father, "I seek you with all my heart; do not let me stray from your commands. I have hidden your word in my heart that I might not sin against you" (Psalm 119:10-11).

READ 2 SAMUEL 5–7.

REFLECT

We've now reached the high point in Israel's history. David is firmly established as king, he has soundly defeated his enemies (5:6-25), brought the ark to Jerusalem (6:1-19), and led the Chosen People into a time of peace unprecedented in the history of Israel before or since (7:1). What would our world be like today if there were more leaders like David? Let's examine the traits he built into his life during his struggle to the top.

David sought God's direction. Notice the phrase, "David inquired of the LORD" (5:19,23). Sometimes Christian leaders have difficulty doing that. When they become prominent, they start to believe their own press reports! But as we've seen with Abraham, Moses, Joshua, Deborah, and others, God is looking for men and women who seek him and follow his direction.

David celebrated God's work. Worship was an active and passionate activity for David (6:14,21). That's because he was so keenly aware of what God had done in his life. If you find your times of worship becoming dry or routine, the solution may not be to find a different church. You may need to get in touch with what God is doing around you. Then you'll have a reason to shout.

David focused on God's priorities. David's prayer (7:18-29) revealed a lot about his "inner self." He was genuinely humble, he knew that God was responsible for his success, and most of all, he showed his understanding of God's "big picture" (7:23).

For all these reasons, David was Israel's greatest king. But his most significant legacy was something else; he became a forerunner of an even greater King who would be born many years later in a little town called Bethlehem.

APPLY

In what areas of your life do you need God's direction most? How do you "inquire of the Lord"? What can you do to celebrate God's work in your life?

PRAY

King Jesus, I worship and praise you with my whole heart today. I want to follow your will for my life, wherever it takes me… *

---

* Now turn to the Review Journal beginning on page 253 to record your key insights from the last five readings.

The Fall of Israel

What goes up must come down. At least that's the way it is for most things. Sadly, it was true for Israel. They had reached glorious heights under the reign of King David. And it looked as if the people God had chosen to be his own had finally made it. They had land, a king, peace, and best of all, a special relationship with the one true God.

But as we shall see in our next five readings, the Israelites couldn't resist the temptation to disobey God's Law and pursue the worship of idols. As a result, God allowed the Babylonians, Israel's ruthless and powerful neighbors, to inflict a severe punishment on them.

But before we get too smug, we must admit that we have the same problem. As the saying goes, "I can resist anything but temptation." It's one of the great lessons of this section that we all need God's help, and the help of fellow Christians, to avoid giving in to sin. And as we'll see, even spiritual leaders need support and honest accountability to avoid the Enemy's traps.

We see this in the lives of three great Bible characters. King David committed adultery and arranged a murder at the pinnacle of his success. God forgave him and continued to use him as his chosen leader, but David bore the consequences of his actions—strife and division in his family—for the rest of his life.

King Solomon, the wisest man who ever lived, experimented with the worship of idols toward the end of his reign. The problem was, he started a pattern of idolatry that got worse and worse with future kings. In the end, God had to put a stop to it. It seemed like such a little thing at first.

And finally, we meet Elijah, one of the most courageous prophets in the Bible. But after a successful showdown with the prophets of Baal, he went AWOL and quit his job for God.

Sin may involve a public fall or a barely noticeable baby step. It may even cause us to run away from God. But the bottom line is, we must always be on our guard. The minute we say, "Well, I'll never do *that* " is when we are most vulnerable to falling.

Reading 36

HOW COULD YOU?

PRAY

You alone, O God, are worthy of praise and honor and glory. I worship you as I come to your Word today...

READ 2 SAMUEL 11:1–12:25.

REFLECT

They say that when a Christian leader falls, it's usually caused by one of two things: money or morals. David didn't seem to have a problem with the former (1 Chronicles 29:2-5). Unfortunately, he seemed to have a weakness with the latter, at least he did in this well-known instance. It's sad but true that a lifetime of positive achievement can be overshadowed by a temporary lapse in judgment.

How could David have done such a thing? How could the man "after God's own heart," the man who showed so much courage in defeating Goliath, the man who exhibited such integrity in resisting Saul's paranoid attempts to kill him, be so quick to commit adultery, arrange a murder, and then abuse his position of power to cover it up?

The answer is the same for David as it is for us today. No matter how strong we may be, all of us have places in our lives that are weak to the pull of sin. That's why the biggest mistake we can make is to forget about sin or think it won't get to us. Often, the time we are most likely to stumble is just after we've made great spiritual progress. That's why it's so important to be part of a Christian community that knows us well enough to hold us accountable. Without that, even the strongest Christian will fall.

Another question that emerges from this passage is, Why was David forgiven and Saul rejected? After all, both sinned against the Lord. The answer comes down to a single word: repentance. When David was confronted with his sin (12:1-10), he immediately and genuinely repented (12:13; see also Psalm 51). Sadly, Saul's response was to rationalize his actions (1 Samuel 13:11-15). It can be incredibly difficult and painful to admit our sin to others and to God. But when we do, God removes the burden and gives us a joy and closeness to him that we can experience in no other way.

APPLY

How do you react when you become aware of sin in your life? Has anyone ever been a "Nathan" in your life? How did you respond to that person?

PRAY

"Search me, O God, and know my heart; test me and know my anxious thoughts. See if there is any offensive way in me, and lead me in the way everlasting" (Psalm 139:23-24).

Reading 37

WISE GUY

PRAY

Heavenly Father, I love your Word, and I eagerly look to it for guidance today. As I do, help me to know and enjoy your presence...

READ 1 KINGS 2–3.

REFLECT

David sure knew how to put the pressure on his son. He publicly praised Solomon's wisdom, then he charged him to settle some old scores for dear old dad (2:5-6). As it turned out, both of these themes played prominently in Solomon's life. There's no denying that a father's vision and encouragement (or lack thereof) can have an enormous impact on the lives of his children.

Solomon is best remembered for his uncommon wisdom (3:16-28). It's significant that although he showed impressive discipline in choosing wisdom over other possibilities (3:9), it was still a gift from God (3:12). Solomon instinctively knew that acknowledging God was the key to genuine understanding (Proverbs 1:7). Today those who would eliminate any discussion of God from learning unwittingly remove the foundation upon which all true knowledge is built.

But Solomon made another choice in this passage that would ultimately lead to the fall of Israel. That choice is summed up in the word "except" (3:3). For all his godly wisdom, Solomon opened the door to the worship of idols, something God clearly hated (Exodus 20:3-6). Often, sin doesn't seem so bad at first. But a series of little steps can take us over the cliff as surely as one big leap.

We can take encouragement from the fact that even some of the Bible's greatest heroes—David and Solomon—had their weaknesses and made sinful choices. But the more encouraging thing is that, even so, God was working out his plan through them. David knew that the secret to staying in tune with that plan is "to walk faithfully before [God] with all [your] heart and soul" (2:4). That's still our challenge and opportunity every day.

APPLY

How would you *honestly* respond if God said to you, "Ask for whatever you want me to give you" (3:5)? Why?

PRAY

Lord God, I've chosen to pursue so many things in my life. But what I want most is to know and follow you. That's what I choose today…

Reading 38

THE HEART OF WORSHIP

PRAY

Lord in heaven, I often feel empty and unable to connect with you. Please fill me with your Spirit so I can worship you today...

READ 1 KINGS 8:1–9:9.

REFLECT

Imagine how the people of Israel felt as they gathered for the dedication of the new temple (8:1-2). For one thing, this was a spectacular building (1 Kings 6:1-38; 7:13-51) and for another, the king was going all out to celebrate (8:5,62-63). But as Solomon and his officials finished the ribbon-cutting ceremony, something spooky happened (8:10). What made this building so special?

Some may have thought it was the ark, which held the stone tablets on which were inscribed the Ten Commandments (8:6-9). The tablets were a tangible reminder of God's work in Israel's past. But the most important thing about this building was that God showed up; he allowed his glory to fill the temple (8:11). It's a powerful example of what true worship is all about.

It's natural to think of worship today in terms of the components of the service itself—the sanctuary, music, preaching, prayers, and communion. But what makes worship come alive is not just how well the service goes; it's how prepared and eager we are to meet the living God. Even a "bad" church service can become good worship if we come with the right hearts. When you go to church, are you expecting God to be there?

Many years later the apostle Peter used the image of the temple to describe the church, that is, all those who have decided to follow Jesus Christ (1 Peter 2:5). Impressive as it was, Solomon's temple was only temporary. It was a preview of a much greater temple, the body of Christ, that will last forever.

At the end of the temple dedication ceremony, God warned the people to remain faithful to him (9:1-9). He knew how quick they'd be to focus on the mechanics of religion and forget about him. But the heart of worship is not so much what we do. It's Who we meet.

Apply

How would you describe your times of worship recently? What makes your worship come alive?

Pray

Lord Jesus, I worship you from my inmost being. You are awesome and holy and loving. Thank you for giving me the opportunity to be part of your new temple...

Reading 39

PROPHETIC SMACKDOWN

PRAY

O Lord, there are so many voices competing for my attention right now. But the one voice I desire to hear most is yours. Open my ears and my heart to your Word today...

READ 1 KINGS 16:29–19:18.

REFLECT

If Solomon opened the door just a crack to idolatry (1 Kings 3:3), Ahab kicked it down. He and his infamous wife, Jezebel, led the people of Israel down an evil path (16:29-33). That's why you have to cheer when Elijah challenged the prophets of Baal to a public smackdown (18:22-24). Are you ready to rumble?

But the sacrifice on Mount Carmel was no pay-per-view event. Elijah rightly saw it as a struggle for the heart and soul of God's people (18:36-37). Throughout history, the church has periodically drifted away from God and his priorities. There are many Christians today who feel as if their denominations are on such a path. It takes wisdom and courage to challenge the church, and we must be careful not to let our egos be the driving force. Of course, the best way to make a difference is through the integrity of our own witness.

But the fascinating thing about this passage is that it introduces us to "two" Elijahs. The first was the bold, fearless prophet who won a dramatic victory for God. The other was a depressed, scared quitter who ran from God (19:1-9). The truth is, serving God is hard work. He allows us to have great successes, but because we are human, we sometimes crash and burn. That's why no matter how strong we are, it's important to take time for rest and renewal (19:7-9).

Ultimately, the thing that will sustain us through the challenges of the Christian life is steady, day-to-day communion with God. That comes from spending time reading his Word, praying, and worshiping with other Christians. Those are the things that can reignite our hearts for the things of God. We should appreciate and remember the "spiritual fireworks" when they happen. But what we need most is the ability to hear God's "gentle whisper" (19:12).

Apply

What spiritual fireworks have you experienced in your Christian life? How have you heard God's gentle whisper lately?

Pray

Heavenly Father, open my eyes to the ways I can be an influence for you in my world. I'm willing to boldly trust you to make a difference through me...

Reading 40

A SEVERE MERCY?

PRAY

Lord, I rejoice in you today. I'm eager to hear what you have to say to me now…

READ 2 KINGS 25.

REFLECT

This is not one of the Bible's most inspirational passages. In fact, it's a pretty depressing picture. Yet it's an important passage because it marks the lowest point in the history of Israel so far. God's people had to learn the hard way that unchecked sin eventually brings devastating consequences. That's still true today.

As a result of Israel's willful pursuit of idols, God allowed the Babylonians to be his instrument of judgment. And they exacted a heavy price, killing Israel's leaders, smashing the glorious temple, burning the city of Jerusalem, and taking most of the people into captivity (25:7-21).

Have you ever experienced a time of overwhelming disaster? Perhaps you've been shocked by the death of a loved one, a sudden financial reversal, or news that you've been diagnosed with a serious disease. How do you react when the bottom drops out?

Sometimes the only way forward is to look back to what God has done in the past—"Lord, I'm miserable. I can't take it anymore, and I see no way out. But you've been good to me in the past, so I'm trusting that you won't abandon me now." Take a minute to read Psalm 74, a prayer written by Asaph, one of those taken into captivity. You'll see that's exactly what he prayed.

If there's anything good about disaster, it's that we are forced to cling more tightly to God, simply because we have no other options. Writer Sheldon Vanauken referred to God's "severe mercy," the fact that God sometimes allows us to experience pain for a loving purpose that we could never see ahead of time (Revelation 3:19). God may shake you, but he won't abandon you. In fact, the very time you feel the lowest may be the time when you are closest to God (Psalm 34:18).

APPLY

What have you learned from the disasters in your life? In what way(s) has God drawn you closer to him through them?

PRAY

Heavenly Father, I'm so thankful that you invite me to cast all my cares on you. Thank you so much for how you care for me (1 Peter 5:7)... *

---

* Now turn to the Review Journal beginning on page 253 to record your key insights from the last five readings.

PSALMS AND PROVERBS

The Bible contains many kinds of writing, and up until now, we've been reading only history—the action-packed accounts of God's people as they became a great nation. Our next five readings, however, introduce us to two new kinds of biblical writing—poetry and wisdom literature.

The psalms are essentially poetry written to express deep truths about God and his world. The person who wrote the most psalms, and many say the best, was King David. Our previous readings have shown us the things David did—both his successes and his failures. But in these three psalms, we get a glimpse of how he felt. And as you'll see, David had an incredible ability to express his feelings, both to us and to God. The book of Psalms reminds us of King David's unique blend of talents; he was a shepherd, a warrior, an administrator, a politician, a spiritual leader, and a poet all in one!

The book of Proverbs, on the other hand, is a collection of wise sayings written primarily by King Solomon. This fascinating book comprises two basic sections: Chapters 1–9 are an extended father-to-son teaching on godly wisdom, while chapters 10–31 are a collection of pithy statements, each expressing a spiritual truth in a memorable way.

The truth is, it's impossible to capture the wonder and richness of the books of Psalms and Proverbs in five short readings. It would be well worth your time to read straight through these wonderful books.

Over the years I've often used a simple pattern for enjoying Psalms and Proverbs throughout the year. In addition to my regular Bible reading plan, if I have extra time I'll read five psalms and one chapter of Proverbs each day. That enables me to read both books in a month. Or whenever I wake up in the middle of the night, unable to sleep, I go downstairs and read the five psalms and one chapter of Proverbs for that day. Often that's enough to redirect my mind and heart to a more peaceful place that allows me to go back to sleep.

So get ready to discover why Psalms and Proverbs have become two of the Bible's most popular books.

Reading 41

NO FEAR!

PRAY

Heavenly Father, I want to focus my heart on you today. I place at your feet all my cares and worries so I can be open to hear your voice...

READ PSALM 23.

REFLECT

I once participated in a group Bible study with people from around the world. We were studying Psalm 23, and the leader asked us to retranslate the opening verse in a way that made sense in our own culture. The responses were very revealing. From Latin America: "The Lord is my friend; he helps me find work for the day." From Russia: "The Lord is my taxi driver; he gets me safely through the streets of Moscow." From Australia: "The Lord is my loving mother; she takes care of me all day long." From India: "The Lord is my guru; he teaches me what I need to know."

David compared the Lord to a shepherd, a job he had personally experienced (1 Samuel 17:34). A shepherd both comforts and protects the sheep (23:2-4). No matter what happens, the shepherd stays with the sheep and actively works for their best interests. Have you experienced those things in your relationship with the Lord? Significantly, Jesus picked up on this image in the New Testament, calling himself the "good shepherd" (John 10:11-18).

But there is a second image in this beloved psalm, one that seems a bit odd at first. David envisioned himself at a banquet table, surrounded by his enemies (23:5). He seemed to be saying that even if the worst happens (23:4), we can trust that God will take care of us (Romans 8:28).

Another time I was part of a group Bible study on Psalm 23 in a prison. One of the inmates told us about his out-of-control life and about the crimes he had committed. From prison he had called his mother in desperation, asking for help. She told him, "I don't know what to tell you, son, except to read Psalm 23." So he did, over and over again. As a result, God worked in his heart, and he accepted Jesus Christ as his Savior and Lord. No matter where you are, no matter what happens, if you've committed your life to the care of the Good Shepherd, you truly have nothing to fear.

APPLY

Take a moment to retranslate the beginning of this psalm, using images from your world. When are you the most aware of the Lord's presence?

PRAY

Dear Lord, you know there are some situations in life that cause me to be fearful. But I ask that you would help me to sense your presence and trust your care so I can face these situations in your strength...

Reading 42

"MEA CULPA"

PRAY

Lord, I enjoy spending time alone with you. Please help me to be completely honest as I listen and speak with you today...

READ PSALM 51.

REFLECT

I once saw a television program where some political commentators we're discussing the impact of a prominent politician's confession of wrongdoing. "He didn't go far enough on the 'grovel-meter,'" one commentator said. "If you're going to grovel, it doesn't work unless you go all the way."

David's confession in this famous psalm certainly goes all the way. The context, as we have studied in a previous reading, is his sin against Bathsheba and her husband, Uriah (2 Samuel 11:2–12:25). Psalm 51 gives us an intimate look into the thoughts and feelings of the "man after God's own heart" after he was confronted with his sin (2 Samuel 12:7,13). By carefully examining David's prayer, we can find three steps to genuine confession.

1. *"Have mercy on me."* (51:1). David didn't rationalize his actions. He honestly described them as "transgressions...iniquity...sin." Ouch. But that's true confession: completely admitting how we've disobeyed God. It makes no sense to hold anything back; God already knows what we've done.

2. *"Cleanse me."* (51:7). David realized that sin is dirty and offensive to God. That's why he used the image of washing to describe forgiveness. We can't remove the stain of sin on our own. Only God can do that.
3. *"Create in me a pure heart."* (51:10). David's heart had been warped by his disobedience. So he asked God to straighten out his inner motives so he'd avoid future sin. After we've sinned, we need time for God to rebuild us from the inside out.

David knew that the worst thing about sin is that it separates us from God (51:11). But he also discovered the joy of putting on the clean clothes of forgiveness and experiencing close fellowship with God once again.

APPLY

Think of a time when you've been overwhelmed by a sense of your own sin. How did you relate to God during that time?

PRAY

"Create in me a clean heart, O God. Renew a right spirit within me. Do not banish me from your presence, and don't take your Holy Spirit from me. Restore to me again the joy of your salvation, and make me willing to obey you" (Psalm 51:10-12, NLT).

Reading 43

PRAISE THE LORD

PRAY

Lord, what a joy it is to spend time with you! I praise you for who you are and for all you've done in my life...

READ PSALM 103.

REFLECT

This is my favorite psalm. Why? Because it touches on so many of the great topics from the Old Testament in twenty-two concentrated verses: justice, Israel's history, God's compassion, forgiveness, human frailty, and more. For me, reading this psalm brings to mind several of the Bible's greatest passages. Perhaps that's what David intended to do when he wrote it.

What makes David's poetry so powerful is that he speaks from the heart about his relationship with God. In doing so, he speaks to things that will deepen our relationship with God today.

The benefits of God. We don't usually think of it this way, but David reminds us that there are some incredible benefits to knowing God (103:3-5). The primary one is forgiveness of our sins. In the New Testament we'll see how God made this possible through the death of Jesus Christ on the cross. But living our lives God's way has positive effects in many areas. In fact, researchers today are discovering that people who pray are healthier. David didn't need an expensive study to figure that one out!

The character of God. What is God like? The main traits David emphasized here are compassion (103:8,13) and a willingness to forgive (103:9-12). That certainly is reassuring. But as Jesus reminded us in his model prayer (Luke 11:2-4), if we want to receive God's forgiveness ourselves, we must be willing to extend it to those around us. That's what godly character is all about.

The response to God. This psalm begins and ends with praise. When you really think about who God is and all he's done for you, what else can you do? I particularly love the phrase "all my inmost being" (103:1). I think of it sometimes when I'm in church. "Heavenly Father, from the depths of my heart and with everything I have, I praise you today." My challenge is to live each day with that kind of response to God.

APPLY

What is your favorite psalm and why? What benefits of knowing God have you experienced?

PRAY

Thank you, heavenly Father, for your compassion and forgiveness. Help me show those qualities to the people around me today...

Reading 44

LIKE FATHER, LIKE SON

PRAY

Lord, I come to you as a child. I'm weak and I don't have all the answers. But I trust that you'll take care of me and give me what I need for this day...

READ PROVERBS 1–4

REFLECT

When I was little, the basement of our house had a bathroom that no one ever used. Then one day I noticed someone had pushed a desk and a chair into the small space between the sink and the shower. On the mirror was a card with a Bible verse printed on it, "Speak [Lord], for thy servant heareth" (1 Samuel 3:10, KJV). I realized that "forgotten" room was the place my father went in the morning, before anyone was out of bed, to read his Bible and pray. That's how he taught me the importance of God's Word.

The book of Proverbs contains the writings of King Solomon, to whom, as we've seen, God gave a unique gift of wisdom (1 Kings 3:5-14). But underneath the all-wise sayings is a father trying to teach his son how to live a godly life (1:8,10,15; 2:1; 3:1). That's the most important job any father will ever have.

Solomon's main point is that wisdom is the foundation for godly living, whether we are a son or a daughter. It's a wisdom that begins with "the fear of the LORD" (1:7; 2:5). Not fear in the sense of panic or dread. Rather, our relationship with God should be characterized by reverence, obedience, and trust. Is that how you relate to God?

Godly wisdom also produces several benefits. It *protects* us against evil and its consequences (1:10-19), and it *provides* us with happiness and health (3:13-26). That's why it's worth pursing. But it's important to note that Solomon is talking about wisdom that is more than just head knowledge. True wisdom is a heart commitment to learn and follow God's ways (4:23).

A wonderful detail in this passage is Solomon's reference to the godly influence of his father and mother—David and Bathsheba (4:3-9). All parents make mistakes, as Solomon's did, but it's never too late to begin teaching our children godly wisdom by our words and example.

APPLY

How would you characterize your relationship with your earthly father? with your heavenly Father? How have you learned about God's wisdom?

PRAY

Heavenly Father, I want to live a life that pleases you. Help me exhibit your wisdom in my words and actions…

Reading 45

A TREASURE CHEST OF WISDOM

PRAY

Lord, there are so many things I need to learn about you and your Word. Show me what you want me to work on most as I read and pray today...

READ PROVERBS 16–18.

REFLECT

When I was growing up, my parents tried several strategies for having "family devotions." What seemed to work best was reading Proverbs after dinner. We went around the table, each person reading one verse aloud until we finished a chapter. Then my mother would ask, "So, which verse stood out to you?" Before we could go outside to play we had to give a *thoughtful* answer. I confess, usually the most "meaningful" verse for me was the last one I read!

Which of these verses was most meaningful to you today? The wonderful thing about the book of Proverbs is that it's like a treasure chest full of little jewels. It's amazing to me today that I still remember many of the proverbs we read around the dinner table. God's Word has a way of sinking in (Psalm 119:11). And what seem like individual verses actually fit together into at least three bigger themes.

Wisdom and folly. When Solomon wrote Proverbs 16:16, he may have been thinking of the choice he made years earlier (1 Kings 3:5-14). Of all the wise things we can do, using our words for positive ends is one of the most significant. Notice how many times Solomon returned to this theme (17:27-28; 18:21). It's hard to read Proverbs without thinking about how we have been using our words.

Humility and pride. Solomon's most famous statement on this theme is Proverbs 16:18. A humble, content life is far more satisfying than grabbing for all the gusto we can get. We all learn this lesson sooner or later. Sadly, sometimes we have to learn it the hard way.

God's will and human action. God expects us to use our talents and abilities, but the paradox is that the final results depend on him (16:1-4). Getting that truth out of balance can tempt us into either inaction or pride. God wants us to act in dependence on him.

APPLY

Try writing out a few proverbs of your own. What wisdom have you gained from your experiences in life and your relationship with God?

PRAY

*"O LORD my God...I am only a little child and do not know how to carry out my duties.... So give your servant a discerning heart...to distinguish between right and wrong" (1 Kings 3:7,9).**

---

* Now turn to the Review Journal beginning on page 253 to record your key insights from the last five readings.

The Prophets

What do you think of when someone says, "He's a prophet for our times"? A longhaired radical with a sign saying THE END IS NEAR? An insightful commentator on social issues? A lone figure courageously standing up to injustice through civil disobedience?

In a sense, the prophets of the Bible were all of those things. They warned of judgment to come, wrote critiques of their society, and, as a result, were forced to stand in opposition to the powers of their day. But there is one other distinguishing factor about biblical prophets: They spoke for God (2 Peter 1:20-21). That's what gave them their greatest power.

Our next five readings introduce us to this new genre of biblical writing: prophecy. The Old Testament includes sixteen prophetic books. They can be categorized in different ways, but the most popular is according to length: the Major Prophets (Isaiah, Jeremiah, Ezekiel, and Daniel) and the Minor Prophets (the last twelve books of the Old Testament with all the strange names!).

Another way to divide the books is by their relationship to a significant historical event: Israel's defeat and exile into Babylon. If a prophet was *pre-exilic* (such as Hosea, Joel, or Amos), he tended to focus on denouncing sin and warning of the coming Day of the Lord. If he was *postexilic* (such as Haggai or Zechariah), he tended to focus on hope and restoration for the broken people of God.

Another fascinating aspect of the prophetic books is the life stories of the prophets themselves. What was it like to be a prophet? We'll read the dramatic personal stories of three of them: Jeremiah, Daniel, and Jonah. As you'll see, being a prophet was a tough, thankless job.

There's one last feature of the prophetic books that you'll want to keep in mind: They often pointed to a coming Messiah, a Savior who would appear many years later. You'll find many such references, but the clearest allusions are in Isaiah 52:13–53:12, which we'll cover in our readings.

The prophetic books are passionate, hard-hitting, and very relevant to our world today. Get ready to be challenged.

Reading 46

THE SUFFERING SERVANT

PRAY

Sovereign Lord, my heart's desire is to draw closer to you. Make me receptive to the specific message you have for me today...

READ ISAIAH 51–53.

REFLECT

When it comes to Old Testament prophets, Isaiah is "the big man on campus." Not only is his book of prophecy the longest, but it is also one of the most quoted in the New Testament. Isaiah's ministry outlasted several kings, both before and after the Exile (Isaiah 1:1), and his writings covered at length two great themes of Old Testament prophecy—warning and judgment (Isaiah 1–39) and hope and salvation (Isaiah 40–66).

Our reading today comes from the hopeful half of Isaiah, a time when God's people were in desperate need of hope. As we've discovered, Israel's idolatry and sin brought terrible punishment (2 Kings 25:1-24). And worst of all, they were afraid God had finally given up on them (Psalm 74:1,9). But God inspired Isaiah with a message of hope that is as relevant today as it was in the eighth century B.C.

God will save his people (51:1–52:12). As the people languished in Babylonian exile, Isaiah pointed to the big picture, what God had done for them in the past (51:1-2). That's a good place to start when you feel you've strayed from God. Next, Isaiah emphasized God's willingness and power to save. That may be hard to believe when you've really messed up, but the truth is, God loves it when sinners return to him (Luke 15:11-32). That's Good News for God's people then and now (52:7).

God will send a Savior (52:13–53:12). The incredible thing about this section—aside from the fact that it was written eight hundred years before Christ!—is the kind of Savior God would send. Not a forceful military conqueror, but a suffering servant, wounded and broken for our transgressions (53:5). The only way for us to be saved, to get rid of our sin problem, is for Someone else to take the punishment for us. And that's exactly what Jesus did on the cross.

Apply

In what areas of your life are you losing hope? How does this passage help? How would you describe God's big picture for you?

Pray

Lord Jesus, I thank you for dying on the cross for me. Your love is so amazing, so overwhelming! I praise you with my whole heart…

Reading 47

WHO, ME?

PRAY

God in heaven, two things overwhelm me today. You are awesome and you care about me. How wonderful it is to know that both are true…

READ JEREMIAH 1:1–3:5.

REFLECT

Jeremiah had a tough assignment. He was young and knew he was a lousy speaker (1:6). Yet God chose him to confront the leaders of his day with a frightening message. No wonder he tried to chicken out. But that's what makes this book so interesting. It combines a powerful message with a candid personal story.

Jeremiah was a young priest, apparently content to fulfill his duties in a small country "parish" (1:1). But God had bigger plans for him, calling him to be "a prophet to the nations" (1:5). It's natural to think that God will use the most talented or successful people to do his work. But that assumes God is dependent on our abilities. In fact, he has the power to do far more than we could ever imagine. All he needs is people who are faithful and willing to follow when he calls.

Notice God's personal interest in Jeremiah (1:5). You may think that God doesn't really know or care about you. But that's not true. The Creator of the universe was thinking about you before you were even born. With a single verse (1:5), God sweeps away the modern debate about when life begins and gives every life—including yours—a God-given purpose.

That doesn't mean life will always be easy. Jeremiah had the difficult task of telling his own people that God was about to unleash a terrible punishment (1:14-16) for their idolatry (1:16; 2:11-19). And what a graphic image he used to describe it—a bride who becomes a prostitute (2:1–3:5). The worst thing about sin is not just that we've broken God's rules. It's that we've broken our relationship with him.

But that's not the end of the story. God's love is so great that he's willing to forgive and "remarry" his wayward people (Jeremiah 31:31-34). As we'll soon discover in our New Testament readings, sending Jesus Christ to earth was God's plan for winning back the hearts of his people (Galatians 4:4-7).

APPLY

What things in life draw you away from God? When do you feel most passionate about your relationship with God?

PRAY

Lord Jesus, forgive me for allowing my heart to value anything more than you. I offer you all my worship, praise, and love...

Reading 48

DARE TO BE A DANIEL

PRAY

"Praise be to the Lord, to God our Savor, who daily bears our burdens" (Psalm 68:19).

READ DANIEL 6.

REFLECT

Our readings in Isaiah and Jeremiah give us the bleak context of this passage in Daniel; Israel's idolatry had produced national defeat and exile for God's people. No doubt many in Daniel's generation would have been tempted to give up, to assume they had no chance in life. But Daniel wasn't worried by his bad circumstances. He made it his number-one priority to develop a deeper relationship with God and then trusted that God would use him however he saw fit (Daniel 1).

As a result, Daniel found himself in a prominent government position (6:1-3). It is interesting that Daniel was perfectly willing to work for a secular king. It's a mistake to think that full-time ministry is the only way to make a difference for God. Certainly God calls some to be pastors and Christian workers. But he calls others to be in the marketplace or government. In fact, people who are willing to boldly live out their faith in secular situations can have a spiritual impact that a full-time Christian worker might not ever have (6:25-27).

But standing up for God brings opposition—in Daniel's case, from jealous bureaucrats (6:4-9). When we face similar attacks in the workplace, they may seem like business as usual. But often they have an element of spiritual opposition behind them. Daniel seems to understand this, since his first reaction was to get away and pray (6:10).

We may never have to face a den of lions for our faith, but we will face opposition. Daniel was willing to sacrifice his career because he trusted God no matter what (6:23). That was the key to his "success" and ours as well.

Apply

What would it mean for you to trust God, no matter what, in your day-to-day work? How could you take more time for private prayer during your day?

Pray

Lord, I want to be a bolder witness for you. Please give me the strength and courage to stand up for you through my words and actions…

Reading 49

BURP!

PRAY

Lord, I'm stepping out of my hectic life into your calm presence. Fill my mind and heart with the things you know I need to hear…

READ JONAH 1–4.

REFLECT

There are many reasons why people take cruises, but Jonah's has to be the most unique. "Guess what? I'm running from the Lord" (1:10). So begins this delightful book that reads more like a four-act play than one of the twelve minor prophets.

Act 1: Running from God. We're too sophisticated today to believe we can run away from God, right? But Jonah's trip to Tarshish was no more ridiculous than when we sin and act as if it's a secret. God knows right away, and eventually others will too (Numbers 32:23). Sin is tricky that way. It causes us to do things we know are not right (1:12; see also Romans 7:7-25) and then convinces us "there's nothing wrong with it" (4:2).

Act 2: Prayer for salvation. Jonah really was swallowed by a great fish (1:17–2:1), and although it gets a big laugh in the Sunday-school play, it must have been a terrifying experience (2:3-6). Coming face to face with the consequences of our sin can be overwhelming. At such times our sin-warped rationalizations are stripped away, and we realize our only hope is to cry out,

"Lord save me!" Jonah's real experience also symbolizes our real need for salvation.

Act 3: Revival in Nineveh. What's encouraging about this chapter is that God gives everyone a second chance. The word of the Lord came "a second time" to Jonah (3:1), reminding us that failing doesn't disqualify us from God's service. Being unwilling to repent does. The Ninevites turned from their wicked ways and believed God. It was the same act of faith that God honored in Abraham (3:5; Genesis 15:6).

Act 4: Disappointment with God. This "play" might have been better if it ended after act 3. But that's not real life; sometimes things happen that cause us to question God. Jonah's temper tantrum gave God yet another chance to demonstrate his patience and love. Some people believe the God of the Old Testament is harsh and unforgiving. But passages such as this show us that God is "a gracious and compassionate God, slow to anger and abounding in love" (4:2).

APPLY

Have you ever been disappointed with God? Why? What restored your trust in him?

PRAY

"But with shouts of praise, I will offer a sacrifice to you, my LORD. I will keep my promise, because you are the one with power to save" (Jonah 2:9, CEV).

Reading 50

GREAT IS THY FAITHFULNESS

PRAY

"I remember the days of long ago; I meditate on all your works and consider what your hands have done" (Psalm 143:5). Thank you, Lord God, for the many things you've taught me about yourself in the Old Testament...

READ MALACHI 1–4.

REFLECT

The book of Malachi is a tough read. It's a blunt exposé of Israel's culture of unfaithfulness in the years following the Exile. After all God had done for his people, they can't seem to resist the temptation to go their own way. (For a quick review of Israel's history, read Psalms 105 and 106.)

We find several examples of this theme in our reading today, but three have particular relevance. First, the Israelites had become insincere in their worship (1:7-14). That's what happens when we try to reduce our relationship with God to a religious routine. Merely going through the motions is offensive to God (1:10) because it shows we're out of touch with the true heart of worship (Deuteronomy 6:4-5).

Second, Malachi singled out men for not remaining committed to their wives (2:10-16). The prophet reminded them of the need to guard both their actions and their spirits (2:15; see also Matthew 5:27-28), a challenge that is especially poignant with the abundant opportunities for sin available on the

Internet. Finally, Malachi hammered his people for their unfaithfulness in the area of tithing—"robbing" is what God calls it (3:8-12). Strong words, considering that only 12 percent of born-again Christians today tithe to the local church and 23 percent give nothing at all. Malachi ends with two full-volume passages on "the Day of the Lord" (2:17–3:5; 4:1-6). Chosen People or not, sin eventually brings judgment.

As we come to the end of the Old Testament, we have to conclude that there has to be a better way for people to relate to God. No matter how hard we try, we can't fix the sin problem on our own. But hang in there. The Good News is coming soon.

Apply

What things weaken your resolve to remain faithful to God? What helps you love God with all your mind, soul, and strength?

Pray

Lord, you have been so faithful to me throughout my life. I want to show my gratitude through the sincerity of my worship and the integrity of my actions… *

---

* Now turn to the Review Journal beginning on page 253 to record your key insights from the last five readings.

Part II

New Testament

The Living Word

Congratulations, you've made it to the halfway point in our journey! After fifty readings through the Old Testament, you are ready to launch into the New Testament. And, of course, the key feature of your next fifty readings is one person, Jesus Christ. In order to help you see the key themes in the New Testament, our readings will skip around a bit. But the main story line remains the same: Jesus came to earth and the church began to grow.

Ever since Adam and Eve sinned in the Garden of Eden, God has been working out his plan of salvation. So far, most of that plan has involved the people of Israel, the Jewish nation. We've seen how God revealed himself to them through signs and wonders in Egypt, through giving them the Law, and most recently, through the message of the prophets. But as we finished the Old Testament, we had the sense that something was still missing. God's people kept falling away from him. They just couldn't get right with God on their own.

That's why he took the dramatic step of sending his own Son, Jesus Christ, to earth. What God had been saying to his people for years and years in a variety of ways, he now says in person (Hebrews 1:1-3). It would be hard to understate the significance of that single event. In fact, the coming of Jesus Christ is the most important moment in all of human history.

But that also introduces the most important question in all of human history, one that every person will eventually have to answer, "Who is Jesus—to me?" (Luke 9:18-27). As you'll immediately see in the next five readings, the New Testament is very clear on the answer. Jesus is God in the flesh (John 1:14), the promised Messiah who has come to earth to save us from our sins (John 1:29-34).

Of course, many people are unwilling to accept what the Bible teaches about Jesus. Perhaps C. S. Lewis offered the best response to such a view in his classic book, *Mere Christianity:*

> I am trying here to prevent anyone from saying the really foolish thing that people often say about Him: "I'm ready to accept Jesus as a great moral teacher, but I don't accept his claim to be God." That is the one thing we must not say. A man who was merely a man and said the sort of things Jesus said would not be a great moral teacher. He would either be a lunatic—on a level with a man who says he is a poached egg—or else he would be the Devil of Hell. You must make your choice. Either this man was and is the Son of God: or else a madman or something worse. You can shut him up for a fool, you can spit at Him and kill Him as a demon; or you can fall at his feet and call him Lord and God. But let us not come with any patronising nonsense about His being a great human teacher. He has not left that open to us. He did not intend to.*

* C. S. Lewis, *Mere Christianity* (New York: Macmillan, 1952), 55-6.

Reading 51

IN THE BEGINNING...AGAIN

PRAY

Heavenly Father, I would like to encounter your Son, Jesus Christ, in a new and real way today...

READ JOHN 1:1-18.

REFLECT

"Okay, there was this 'man' named Jesus, and I'm writing this to tell you about all the really great things he did." That's how I would have started my gospel account. But not John; he started way above the clouds (1:1-5), before time, before Creation, before anything.

His opening phrase, "In the beginning..." (1:1) parallels the first verse of Genesis. John wanted us to know that the coming of Jesus was as significant as the creation of the world; it was literally the start of a new creation (2 Corinthians 5:17). He used a somewhat mysterious term, "the Word" (1:1), to describe Jesus. The point is, what God had been saying to humankind from a distance for so many years—through creation, through his signs and wonders on behalf of Israel, through the Law and the Prophets—he now says through the Person of Christ. Jesus Christ was God himself (1:1,14), the Living Word. If you want to know what God is like, look at Jesus.

The sad part was, people just didn't get it; they didn't understand who Jesus really was (1:5,10). That's still true today. Many accept him as a good man or a great moral teacher or even a unique model of team building and leadership. But unless you also accept him as God himself (1:14), it's the same thing as rejecting him (1:11).

The Good News is that God loves us and, through Jesus, has made a way for all people to become his children (1:12). No longer is our relationship with God dependent on sacrifices or keeping a detailed set of laws, as we saw in the Old Testament (1:17). All God wants us to do is receive and believe Jesus. That's how we can discover the incredible blessings God wants to give us (1:16-17)—the best being an eternal relationship with him.

APPLY

Would you say that you have received and believed Jesus? Explain.

PRAY

Heavenly Father, it's mind-boggling to think that you came to this earth because you wanted a relationship with me. Please draw me closer to you today...

Reading 52

GREETINGS!

PRAY

"My soul glorifies the Lord and my spirit rejoices in God my Savior, for he has been mindful of the humble state of his servant" (Luke 1:46-48).

READ LUKE 1.

REFLECT

It must have been an exciting family gathering when Elizabeth and Mary met (1:39-40). Not only were both women pregnant as a result of miraculous circumstances, but both realized that God had chosen them for something special. God often uses unlikely people to do his work. You may feel too old, like Elizabeth (1:18), or too insignificant, like Mary (1:48). But God can do incredible things (1:37) through people who are faithful and humbly dependent on him (1:6,13,50). No matter where you are in life, God can use you if you've developed those qualities.

But when God chooses us, we must be ready to respond. Compare Zechariah's "How *can* I be sure of this?" (1:18, emphasis added), to Mary's "How *will* this be?" (1:34, emphasis added). Mary believed God could do it; Zechariah wasn't so sure. Having faith doesn't mean you will understand exactly what God is doing in your life. Very often, you won't. Faith is simply believing that God has the power to do anything (1:37) and then committing yourself to his way, no matter what happens (1:38).

Sometimes the life of faith can lead us down a lonely road. We can become discouraged, wondering if anyone notices our attempts to follow God. But Gabriel pulled back the curtains of heaven and gave us a wonderful glimpse of God personally listening to our prayers (1:13) and taking note of our attempts to live for him (1:28-30). Living the Christian life can be a challenge, but the encouraging thing is, you are never alone (Hebrews 12:1).

Gabriel's primary job was to announce that God was ready to make the big move in his plan of salvation (1:30-35). We've been following that plan since Adam and Eve first sinned in the garden. The exciting thing about the New Testament is that God steps into history and makes the plan happen himself. That's the Big Story.

APPLY

Do you ever feel isolated or discouraged in your attempts to follow God? When and why? What makes you feel that God cares about you?

PRAY

Heavenly Father, it's true that I sometimes don't understand what you are doing in my life. But I believe you have the power to do incredible things through me, and I'm ready if you want to use me today...

Reading 53

CHRISTMAS SPECIAL

PRAY

"Hark! the herald angels sing, 'Glory to the newborn King.'" Lord, no matter what day of the year it is, I'm so thankful for what you did for me on that first Christmas...

READ LUKE 2:1-40.

REFLECT

Whenever I read this passage, I can't help thinking about the classic Charlie Brown Christmas special on television, where Linus walks onto an empty stage and recites from the second chapter of Luke. He ends by saying simply, "That's what Christmas is all about, Charlie Brown." The show-stopping truth is that God came to earth.

It's incredible to think that the Savior of the world would make his entrance in this way: an inconvenient, messy birth in a stable (2:6-7). That's no way to get good ratings—or to get noticed at all. But God intentionally chose to work his greatest miracle through "invisible" people like some overwhelmed parents and terrified shepherds.

It's a mistake to assume that God prefers using media stars and prominent people to accomplish his purposes. That's a danger for those of us who live in the Western world. Even in our local churches, we sometimes act as if the clergy are the only ones through whom God can work. Certainly, God has given pastors and other Christian leaders a special and important calling (1 Timothy 3:1-13). But the healthiest churches are those that encourage everyone, regardless of their position or natural abilities, to use their spiritual gifts for the benefit of all (1 Corinthians 12:1-31).

Look what happened to the shepherds. Smelly and bungling, they seemed more like the Three Stooges than ambassadors for God. What did they know about prophecy or God's plan of salvation? All they knew is that their lives had been changed by an incredible time of worship (2:13-14) and an opportunity to meet Jesus (2:15-16). That experience transformed them into effective evangelists who had a powerful impact for God (2:17). And that's what the church is all about, Charlie Brown.

Apply

Would you say that Jesus has transformed your life? Why do you think so? How has he done this?

Pray

Lord Jesus, I worship and praise you today. Please give me the courage and ability to spread the word about what you've done in my life…

Reading 54

THE WORLD'S GREATEST PROPHET

PRAY

Lord, please prepare my heart so that I may receive with joy what you have to say to me today...

READ LUKE 3:1-20.

REFLECT

John the Baptist was a quintessential biblical prophet. He lived in the desert (3:2), ate natural food, and wore rough clothes (Matthew 3:4). But the most important thing about him was that "the word of God came to him" (Luke 3:2). As we discovered in our Old Testament readings, God called prophets to the difficult task of announcing his message of both judgment and hope.

But John the Baptist had an extra assignment; he was to prepare the way for the Messiah (3:4). As it turned out, the Anointed One was his cousin Jesus. John the Baptist deserves credit for recognizing God's work in a member of his family. It's sometimes difficult to encourage the spiritual growth in our siblings or extended family because we know what they are "really like." But your family members are the ones you're the closest to in life and the ones on whom you can have the biggest spiritual influence. That may require an intentional "reprogramming" of your family habits or patterns so that you'll be better able to affirm God's work in their lives.

John had a big influence on Jesus. Notice the main elements of his message: a call to repentance and a challenge to "produce fruit," all in preparation for the coming of the Christ (3:7-14). Later in his own ministry, Jesus preached his famous "six woes" sermon (Luke 11:37-54), which had the same tone and many of the same words and themes as John the Baptist's message here. Jesus even went so far as to say that John the Baptist was the greatest prophet (Luke 7:24-28).

In the end, John devoted his life to the higher purpose of humbly pointing people to Jesus (3:15-17; see also John 3:27-36). You may not be a gutsy prophet or a fiery preacher, but you can still have a big impact for God by letting your words and actions point others toward Jesus. And that begins with your family.

Apply

In what ways could you influence your family members to embrace God's priorities? Would any of your family patterns have to change in order to accomplish this? How has your family influenced your faith?

Pray

Lord God, sometimes I feel like "a voice calling in the desert." But with your help, I'll stand up for you in my family, work, and community...

Reading 55

LEAD US NOT INTO TEMPTATION

PRAY

Heavenly Father, I am so grateful for your love. Feed me from your Word today so that I may live a life that pleases you...

READ MATTHEW 3:13–4:17.

REFLECT

Why did Jesus need to be baptized by John? They both knew he didn't need it. After all, Jesus was the Son of God and without sin. So John's baptism of repentance was unnecessary. The key is found in the word *fulfill* (3:15). Jesus' mission was to take the sin of the world—including yours and mine—on himself (John 1:29). His life on earth was devoted to fulfilling that mission, and as a result, he received the affirmation of his heavenly Father (3:17).

What a shock it must have been for Jesus to go directly from the close fellowship with God to the traps Satan had prepared in the desert (4:1). But following a time of spiritual growth—or even *during* a time of spiritual growth—is often when the Enemy chooses to pounce. Your temptations may not be as dramatic as the ones Jesus faced. You may simply be tempted to express angry words to your spouse or colleagues in a weak moment, to pursue an unhealthy relationship when you are tired and needy, or even to become proud about your spiritual progress. But if you're growing in your relationship with God, watch out. Satan will try to disrupt you and convince you that you're a spiritual phony. Perhaps that's why even Jesus got away for a time of prayer after periods of intense spiritual activity (Mark 1:35).

It's helpful to notice what Jesus did to avoid Satan's temptations. Each time, Jesus went back to the Word of God, the Bible. It gave him the solid ground he needed to make the right choices (4:4). The same is true for us today. Notice, too, that the Bible can protect us, as it did Jesus. But it can also mislead us if we misuse it, as Satan attempted to do (4:5-6). That's why it's important to be part of a Christ-centered, Bible-believing church. It's much easier to stay on track when you are accountable to a faithful community of fellow Christians. Don't try to walk through the desert by yourself.

APPLY

When do you feel closest to God? When are you most susceptible to temptation? What steps could you take to prepare for the temptations that will come your way this week?

PRAY

Lord, there are temptations all around me. Forgive me for the many times I've given in. With the help of your Word and your Spirit, I intend to please you with my words and actions today… *

---

* Now turn to the Review Journal beginning on page 253 to record your key insights from the last five readings.

THE TEACHINGS OF JESUS

Imagine you were alive when Jesus was on earth. And imagine you had the opportunity to hear him teach—perhaps you were on the hillside when he preached the Sermon on the Mount, or you were in the crowd when he told one of his insightful parables. Now imagine that you have come home for the night, and as you enter the house, someone in your family says, "So what'd he say?" How would you summarize the teachings of Jesus?

That's the impossible challenge we now have, to capture the essence of Jesus' teachings in five short readings. But as you'll see, Jesus was always teaching, because he knew that his actions spoke as loudly, if not louder, than his words.

For example, one of our readings in this section includes the Lord's Prayer (Matthew 6:9-13). But Jesus' most powerful teaching on prayer may not have been this model prayer. Instead, it was his lifestyle of prayer. Notice that this is what triggered the disciples' interest in prayer (Luke 11:1). As we read the Gospels, we find frequent references to Jesus' pattern of prayer (Mark 1:35).

Jesus preached what he practiced, and that's one thing that gave him credibility as a teacher. Of course, the other thing—the main thing—was the fact that he was God in the flesh. His listeners didn't understand that yet. But the more he taught, the more they realized that he was unique (Matthew 7:28-29).

Our readings focus on two other methods Jesus used for his teaching: preaching and parables. The Sermon on the Mount is unquestionably the greatest sermon ever preached. Jesus delivered it early in his public ministry just as he was starting to gain "traction in the polls." Instead of giving the crowds feel-good messages, he gave them a full dose of his moral and ethical teaching that called people to the highest possible standard (Matthew 5:48). Jesus never dumbed down his message.

The second teaching method Jesus used was parables. Telling stories about common things and the familiar situations of life helped him connect with his listeners. It also enabled him to point out the hypocrisy and sin of the religious leaders who opposed him without seeming overly confrontational.

Preaching and storytelling combined with a consistent lifestyle was Jesus' masterful formula for getting his point across.

Reading 56

RADICAL HAPPINESS

PRAY

"May the words of my mouth and the meditation of my heart be pleasing in your sight, O LORD, my Rock and my Redeemer" (Psalm 19:14).

READ MATTHEW 5:1–6:4.

REFLECT

When people think about the Sermon on the Mount today, they often refer to it as the Beatitudes, that is, the nine "blessed" statements Jesus made at the opening of this passage (5:3-12). The word *beatitude* means "blessed" or, literally, "happy." In other words, Jesus began the world's greatest sermon by defining true happiness. Sounds like a winner.

The problem is, the only people he talked about were losers—the poor in spirit, mourners, the meek and persecuted. No one wants to be around people like that. But according to Jesus, the way to be happy is to go out of our way to include those who are troubled. Jesus loved the down-and-outer, and if we want to be his followers, so should we.

Next Jesus tackled another touchy subject: influencing others (5:13-16). Today many people believe that the most important thing about religion is keeping it private. For them, privacy is more essential than truth. But Jesus challenged his followers to be like *salt*—flavoring and preserving the world with the gospel—and *light*—demonstrating the gospel with godly actions.

Once you've discovered "the way and the truth and the life" (John 14:6), there's no way to keep it hidden (5:14-15). As Saint Francis once said, "Preach the gospel all the time. Use words when necessary."

Jesus continued by taking aim at some even tougher topics such as murder, adultery, divorce, and revenge (5:21-47). In each case he referred to the teachings of the Law ("You have heard that it was said…") and then raised the stakes by zeroing in on the source of the problem: the heart (5:28). Following a list of rules does no good without a heart that has the right motivation—reconciliation, faithfulness, forgiveness, and love. These are the things Jesus valued most.

Apply

What makes you happy? Which part of the Sermon on the Mount is most challenging to you? Why?

Pray

Lord, "the pursuit of happiness" takes up a lot of my time and energy. Help me cultivate a heart that truly pleases you…

Reading 57

THE AUDIENCE OF ONE

PRAY

Lord God, you already know everything I need for this day. So I begin this time with you by worshiping and praising you. What an incredible, loving, awesome God you are...

READ MATTHEW 6:5–7:29.

REFLECT

You can tell that Jesus never went to seminary. If he had, he would have begun his sermon with a joke, covered three points, and ended with a poem. But Jesus was on a mission; he had three short years to communicate everything his heavenly Father wanted him to say to the world. And after that, he faced the cross. So he packed everything in.

One of his most important teachings was about prayer. The Lord's Prayer (6:9-13) is undoubtedly the world's most famous prayer. It combines two perspectives that can help us today. First, in prayer we look beyond ourselves to God, his nature, his holiness, his kingdom, and his will. Second, we focus on our day-to-day issues—food, forgiveness, and strength to avoid temptation. At the very least, prayer involves worshiping and requesting. Without a balance of these two perspectives, our prayers become lopsided and eventually less effective.

But for Jesus, prayer wasn't just a verbal formula. It was the natural extension of a lifestyle focused on doing his Father's will. Notice how often Jesus referred to "your Father" in the second half of this sermon (6:6,8,18,32, etc.). Whether he was talking about prayer or fasting or giving or any other subject, the point is, we are to do all things with our heavenly Father in mind. Or as writer Os Guinness has put it, we are to play to "the audience of One." When God becomes the central focus of our lives, things like money, possessions, clothes, or food all take their proper place (6:33).

Jesus concluded his Sermon on the Mount with more straight talk: forgive or else (6:14-15), don't judge others (7:1-6), and watch out for false prophets (7:15-20). He even saved his toughest word for the end: "Not everyone who says to me, 'Lord, Lord,' will enter the kingdom of heaven, but only he who does the will of my Father who is in heaven." (7:21,22-23). There's a big difference between feeling good and being blessed (Matthew 5:3-12).

APPLY

What do you suppose Jesus would have to say to people walking through a modern-day shopping mall?

PRAY

Conclude your time here by slowly reading the Lord's Prayer aloud, stopping to reflect on each phrase of the prayer.

Reading 58

D-DAY FOR SIN

PRAY

Lord, there are so many things that prevent your Word from taking root in my life. Help me set them aside so that I may receive your Word today…

READ MATTHEW 13.

REFLECT

On the stormy morning of June 6, 1944, the United States, Great Britain, and their allies began a massive effort to liberate Europe from the grip of Nazi Germany. At great sacrifice of human life, the Allied forces invaded the beaches of Normandy, France, and over the next year gradually reclaimed the captured territory and defeated the enemy regime.

D-day provides a perfect picture of the kingdom of heaven. Ever since Adam and Eve disobeyed God in the Garden of Eden, the world has been under the influence of sin. But when Jesus "invaded" the earth, it was the beginning of the end for Satan's evil empire. Theologians describe the kingdom of heaven as "the rule of God's grace in the world." As Jesus went about his public ministry, he liberated more and more people from sin and expanded his kingdom on earth. And through his death on the cross, he opened the way for everyone to enter his kingdom.

But that was a hard concept for people to see at the time, which is why Jesus used so many common analogies. By comparing the kingdom of heaven to things like yeast, hidden treasure, a mustard seed, and a net, Jesus painted a picture of a seemingly insignificant thing that would have an overwhelming impact. That's how it is when we decide to follow Jesus—it seems like a small step at first, but over time it changes everything about our lives, both now and for eternity.

We must be careful, however, not to allow our consideration of the kingdom of heaven to become a mere intellectual exercise. Jesus challenged his hearers to "understand with their hearts" (13:15). That means we allow his Word to sink in and affect our attitudes, motivations, and actions. Inhabitants of God's kingdom are committed to being both hearers and doers of his Word (James 1:22-25).

APPLY

How has it changed your life to be in God's kingdom? Have you taken the first step yet?

PRAY

Heavenly Father, thank you so much for inviting me into your kingdom. I want to allow your Word to sink deeper and deeper into my heart so that I can bear fruit for you...

Reading 59

THE UNCOMMON DEED

PRAY

Holy Spirit, I invite you to be present with me as I explore this passage. Please reveal the things I need to know for this day…

READ LUKE 10:25-37.

REFLECT

This passage has special significance to me since my home church is called The Church of the Good Samaritan. In the narthex (the western entrance), we have a life-size, contemporary statue of one person helping another person up, poignantly symbolizing this parable and our church's motto, "Doing the uncommon deed in the name of Jesus Christ."

On the surface the man in this passage asked a thoughtful question about the next life: "What must I do to inherit eternal life?" (10:25). But he wasn't completely satisfied with Jesus' answer, so he pressed for a guarantee (10:29). At times we, too, feel the tendency to reduce God's *agape* love to a mere formula. But it doesn't work that way. If your relationship with God is too heavily defined by a list of dos and don'ts, you'll have trouble being passionate in your love for God or joyful in your service to others. Jesus didn't seem too interested in the man's "perceived" need either. Instead, he zeroed in on the real need, using the well-known parable from which we notice at least two principles.

First, *the outcast was the hero.* No one liked or respected Samaritans, but Jesus was saying that the outcast is able to understand and express God's love better than anyone else, including the religious experts. Christian faith is not about being an expert or being perfect all the time. It's about being willing to receive God's love and forgiveness and then being able to express those realities to those around us.

The second principle, as well as the punch line of the story, is that *true neighbors are those who show mercy.* The word *mercy* carries with it both the idea of a feeling of empathy and compassion as well as taking action on behalf of those who are helpless. A Christian who has all the right answers but does not show mercy is not an effective witness for God (Luke 6:36).

APPLY

Who needs mercy from you? How could you express it to this person today?

PRAY

Lord God, thank you for showing incredible mercy to me. With your help, I intend to do the same for others today…

Reading 60

SINNERS WELCOME

PRAY

Lord Jesus, I want to draw closer to you today. Please give me a deeper understanding of why you died on the cross for me...

READ LUKE 15.

REFLECT

I once saw a cartoon that showed two clergymen scowling at a third as he strode purposefully into his crowded church. The one scowling cleric said to the other, "Yes, but it's the *way* he saves souls that makes my blood boil!"

It's easy for Christian leaders to feel the kind of professional jealousy and theological snobbery that we see in our passage today (15:1-2). But we can get off track, too, when we view the church as a club for those who have it all together—or at least, who think they do. Jesus' image of the church was more like a lost-and-found bin. That's the point of the stories about the lost sheep and the lost coin (15:3-10). The whole reason Jesus came was to reclaim lost and broken people. The Pharisees just didn't get it.

In his third story (15:11-32), Jesus gave us a glimpse into God's heart—he loves sinners and is waiting for them to return to him. You'd think the father would have taken his prodigal son to the woodshed, or at least have scolded him, before welcoming him back. But contrary to what we think, God is far more interested in repentance than punishment. In fact, Jesus defined true repentance when he passionately quoted the younger brother (15:17-19). Is that how you feel when you recognize your own sin?

You have to feel sorry for the resentful older brother. For him, the father's love should be reserved only for the few who earned it—especially him. But if that's how God felt, no one would be saved. The mission of the church of Jesus Christ is not to isolate the "good" people, it's to welcome and save the "bad" people, which includes you and me and everyone else. That's the kind of church that makes God really, really happy (15:21-24).

APPLY

Think of a time when you truly repented from the heart. How did that experience make you feel about God? Do you ever try to earn God's love? How?

PRAY

Heavenly Father, forgive me for being like the older brother. You've been so generous with your love for me. Help me share some of that love with the struggling people around me… *

---

* Now turn to the Review Journal beginning on page 253 to record your key insights from the last five readings.

THE MIRACLES OF JESUS

I used to love Woody Allen films. He's famous for making comedies that portray hapless bumblers (with himself playing the lead) struggling with the questions of life, death, and God. In one film Allen sarcastically says, "If I could only see a real miracle, then I could believe." But Woody Allen's characters never believe; they just keep searching. Now I have trouble watching Woody Allen films because I wonder if he even wants to find the answer. For me, there's no humor in a dead end.

As we'll discover in our next five readings, seeing is not always believing. Jesus performed all kinds of miracles. He healed lame and blind people, walked on water and changed the weather, exorcised demons and brought dead people back to life. This led many to put their faith and trust in him. But it also caused many others, like the religious leaders, to oppose him. The fact is, if we've already decided not to believe, no amount of proof will change our minds.

Author and speaker Josh McDowell is another person who wrestled with the questions of life, death, and God. He, too, went on a search for answers, only he was more honest about his assumptions. McDowell set out to prove that Jesus was not divine and that Christianity was bogus. He researched and studied everything he could. He lined up enormous amounts of data. But in the end he concluded that his original assumption was wrong. The evidence pointed to one conclusion: Jesus Christ was who he claimed to be—Son of God, Savior, and Lord of all.

In his book *Evidence That Demands a Verdict,* McDowell notes that a well-known philosopher—Sören Kierkegaard—compared faith to a "leap in the dark." But after honestly evaluating the data, Josh McDowell said that, for him, coming to faith in Jesus Christ was like "a leap into the light."

Jesus linked his teaching with miracles (Matthew 4:23) and instructed his disciples to do the same (Luke 9:1-2). It was a powerful combination. But the biggest miracle of all was when he himself came back to life after dying on the cross for our sins. That's the big miracle that validated everything he said and did.

Reading 61

ALL YOU CAN EAT

PRAY

"Blessed Lord, who hast caused all holy Scriptures to be written for our learning: Grant that we may in such wise hear them, read, mark, learn, and inwardly digest them." (The Book of Common Prayer)

READ LUKE 9:1-36.

REFLECT

Any politician (or youth group leader) can tell you the secret to attracting a large crowd: free food. But Jesus was no politician, and his miraculous feeding of five thousand men (not to mention many more women and children who were undoubtedly present) had tremendous significance both for the disciples and for us.

To fully understand this miracle, we must consider its context. As we have already discovered, Jesus had been preaching about the kingdom of heaven (Matthew 13). He then sent the disciples out with the same message (9:1-2). "You've seen how I do it, now you give it a try." Some people today are offended by the idea of evangelism. But Jesus didn't ask his followers to impose a set of personal beliefs on others. He simply asked them to heal people and share the Good News (9:6).

When the disciples returned, Jesus took them aside for fellowship and debriefing (9:10), a good idea for those involved in ministry. And that's when he chose to feed the large crowd. It would be nice to know how it happened. Did a stack of loaves drop out of the sky? Did the bread miraculously replenish itself as people pulled off pieces? The text only says, "They all ate and were satisfied" (9:17). But the point is, Jesus had given his followers an unforgettable symbol of what he had been teaching them: God's kingdom multiplies as it is given away.

This miracle also demonstrated another important truth: Jesus really was the Son of God. Peter understood sooner than anyone else (9:20). And about a week later, God confirmed it for Peter, John, and James in the quintessential "mountaintop experience" (9:28-36). Jesus didn't miraculously create food to attract a crowd. He did it to drive home an important message: "I am God in the flesh. I am here to establish a kingdom that must grow. I need you to tell others all about it."

APPLY

How do you feel about sharing God's Good News with others? Explain. Who needs to hear the Good News from you?

PRAY

Heavenly Father, you've given me so much through your Son, Jesus Christ. With your help, I'm ready to share that Good News with others...

Reading 62

IMAGINATIVE FAITH

PRAY

Lord Jesus, my mind and heart are full of the pressures and problems of life. But I set them aside now so that I can spend some time seeking your face...

READ MATTHEW 14:22-36.

REFLECT

Several years ago I was involved in a situation that caused me great stress. The problem was so big that I thought I'd never get out of it. At my lowest point I read this passage and taped a copy of Jesus' words to the wall beside my desk. After that, whenever I felt fearful I'd say this verse aloud: "Take courage! It is I. Don't be afraid" (14:27). It took several years, but God miraculously resolved my problem.

Some people act as if becoming a Christian exempts them from life's problems. Unfortunately, that's not true. But no matter how bad things get, God never abandons us. If we are willing to reach out to him, the moment of crisis can become the time of closest fellowship with our Lord.

A lot has been made of Peter's lack of faith on the lake (14:30-31), but I'm impressed with his imagination under such pressure. I would never have imagined that I could walk on water; I would have stayed in the boat. Sometimes faith requires imagination, the willingness to believe that God has the ability to do things that seem impossible (Matthew 19:26). That doesn't mean God will give us everything we wish for. It simply means we can trust that God will provide everything we need, when we need it, if we stay focused on him.

With all the drama of the storm, let's not miss what Jesus was doing before he walked on the water; he was spending "quality time" with his heavenly Father (14:23). It would have been easy for Jesus to let his early successes go to his head (14:13-21) or to be overwhelmed by the pressures of ministry (14:22-36). That's why he needed to spend time alone in prayer. And if Jesus needed prayer to stay spiritually focused and renewed, we need it even more.

APPLY

What are your biggest problems? What makes you fearful? What could you do to seek God in the midst of your storms?

PRAY

Lord, you know there are some problems in my life that I'd love for you to solve. But even more than that, I want to experience your presence. That's my prayer today...

Reading 63

I SEE WHAT YOU MEAN

PRAY

"As the deer pants for streams of water, so my soul pants for you O God. My soul thirsts for God, for the living God" (Psalm 42:1-2).

READ JOHN 9.

REFLECT

Sometimes people who are the most religious are also the most resistant to a genuine work of God. That's what we see in this passage. After hearing about the miraculous healing of a blind man (9:6-7), the religious leaders responded with skepticism. The problem was, they were more interested in their rules than in the reality of what God had done (9:16).

What causes good people to resist God's work? Sometimes it's fear of the unknown or a legitimate desire to avoid being misled. But we should be careful if we feel a resistance to spiritual things just because they do not fit our way of thinking. Sometimes the most honest thing we can say is, "This is outside my experience, but I'm open to whatever God wants to show me" (see Acts 5:38-39). That kind of honesty can open the door to a deeper understanding of God.

The disciples tried to overthink the blind man's predicament (9:1-2). There are still people who say sin is the cause of sickness. Sometimes it can be. But Jesus reminds us that God has reasons for allowing things that aren't always apparent to us (9:3-5), and that's good news for those experiencing illness or disease today. How might that affect the way you pray for your loved ones?

In the midst of all the arguing, the blind man had the clearest insight of all. Note the progression of his faith. He started with a basic understanding of the facts (9:11,25), formed an opinion about Jesus (9:17), but finally made a decision to believe (9:38) in spite of the consequences (9:34). That's a good description of how to become a Christian. Jesus welcomes the tough questions of honest seekers (9:35-37). But to those who use their doubts as a way of avoiding the truth, he is not so patient (9:39,41).

Apply

How would you trace the progression of your personal faith? What questions do you have about Jesus? Who could help you sort them out?

Pray

Lord Jesus, thank you for opening my eyes to the truth about you. Help me to share that truth with others through my words and actions…

Reading 64

IN THE NAME OF JESUS

PRAY

Lord, you are powerful and mighty and above all things. And yet you know and love me. I thank you for that today...

READ MARK 5:1-20.

REFLECT

Whenever I drive past a pornography shop or a psychic reader's place of business, I become aware of the reality of evil. At such times I'll often sing a song my mother taught me when I was a child: "In the name of Jesus, by the power of God...in the name of Jesus, by the power of God...in the name of Jesus, by the power of God...the Enemy flees, the Enemy flees." It's my way of claiming God's protection and announcing his authority over evil.

The demon-possessed man in our passage knew the reality of evil (5:1-5), and it was destroying his life. That's Satan's agenda—to capture and destroy God's creation. Some people think the devil is funny. But evil is no joke, and we are all vulnerable to attack (1 Peter 5:8). But for all his destructive powers, Satan knows who the higher power really is. When Jesus came to earth, Satan was defeated, and he knows it (5:6-7).

You'd think the people would have cheered when Jesus healed the demon-possessed man. No more howling at night, no more danger to the community. But they weren't happy; they were afraid (5:15). Why? Perhaps they were more comfortable with the status quo. "Oh, that's just how he is." But Jesus wants to bring the most radical kind of healing into our lives. He wants to break our addiction to sin. And that can be unsettling.

Jesus also wants to empower us to share the Good News. Notice that he didn't spend time teaching the formerly demon-possessed man. He didn't need to. All he told him was, "Go…tell them how much the Lord has done for you, and how he has had mercy on you" (5:19). A changed life is still the clearest and most powerful statement of the gospel there is.

APPLY

In what ways, if any, have you become addicted to sin? What can you do to open yourself to God's radical healing power in your life?

PRAY

Lord Jesus, I invite you into those places in my life where the Enemy still has a grip. Please free me from the chains that hold me, so that I may serve you with my whole heart…

Reading 65

DEAD MAN WALKING

PRAY

Lord, I don't like to think about death. But as I explore your Word today, give me a new appreciation for how you've overcome death and offered me new life...

READ JOHN 11.

REFLECT

As far as the religious leaders were concerned, this miracle was the straw that broke the camel's back. When Jesus brought Lazarus back to life, the chief priests and Pharisees decided they had to kill Jesus (11:53). What made this miracle so threatening to the religious establishment?

The answer is simple: politics. The leaders feared anything that would cause the Romans to take away the symbols of their national identity (11:48). Allowing ourselves to value anything more than the one true God—even good things like church and country—can have disastrous implications. Our world is full of wars that are the result of this very mistake.

But Jesus didn't care much about politics. He cared about people. One feature that stands out in this passage is the compassion of Jesus. He really loved people (11:3,5,36). And what an impact his love had on Martha. In an earlier encounter with Jesus, Martha had come off as a fussy complainer (Luke 10:38-42). Here she's the first one to respond to him (11:20). Unlike the religious leaders, Martha had put Jesus at the center of her life and priorities.

But there was a deeper reality to this miracle. Jesus knew he was going to die and that God would bring him back to life. By raising Lazarus he created an unforgettable symbol of the new life, eternal life, that he would offer to those who believed in him (11:25-26). The irony is that the religious leaders made this very point without realizing it (11:50). How sad that people can go to church all their lives and still not understand who Jesus is. Martha didn't understand everything either, but she honestly stated what she did understand (11:24) and then entrusted herself and her future to Jesus (11:27). That's all he asks us to do.

APPLY

What about Jesus threatens you, if anything? What, if anything, do you love more than Jesus?

PRAY

Yes, Lord, I believe you are the Christ, the Son of God. And I believe you are the resurrection and the life. Thank you for offering that new and eternal life to me… *

---

* Now turn to the Review Journal beginning on page 253 to record your key insights from the last five readings.

THE CROSS OF CHRIST

The cross is the most recognized and reproduced symbol in the history of the world. Not only does it appear in spiritual settings—on stained-glass windows, in Bibles, and in prayer books—but it also has secular popularity, being worn as jewelry or used as a "lucky charm" for the car mirror. Why is the cross so important? Of course, the main reason is that it represents Jesus Christ's death on a cross. That single event was literally the intersection of time and eternity. It was on the cross that Jesus died for the sins of the world, thereby making a way for all people to have a relationship with God, one that would last forever.

But the broad popularity of this symbol has perhaps blurred the horror of how the cross was originally used. When Jesus was on earth, the Romans used crucifixion as a way of punishing criminals or humiliating enemies of the state. Either way, it was a gruesome form of public execution. Victims were usually whipped first and forced to carry a crossbeam to the place of execution. They were then nailed to the beam, which was hoisted up onto a stake. Death was a slow, agonizing process and usually came from loss of blood or suffocation. A modern symbol that captures some of the horror of the cross is the electric chair, although no one would consider wearing that as jewelry.

Jesus knew exactly what he was in for (Luke 9:22). And even though his mission on earth was to die on the cross, it was still a struggle (Mark 14:32-42). But he did it first because it was his Father's will and second because it was the only way to pay the price for sin, once and for all. Without the Cross there could be no salvation.

Jesus never intended the cross to be a fashion statement. For him, it was a symbol of his followers' all-out commitment to him. As he said, "Anyone who does not carry his cross and follow me cannot be my disciple" (Luke 14:27). As you'll see in the rest of the New Testament, the early church clearly understood the significance of the Cross (Romans 6:5-11; Galatians 2:20; Philippians 2:5-11).

Your next five readings take you to the very heart of God's plan of salvation. It's the Big Story we've been following through the Bible. Take some time to prayerfully reflect on the meaning of the Cross for you.

Reading 66

A MEAL TO REMEMBER

PRAY

Lord Jesus, you are the Bread of Life (John 6:25-40). Please fill my hunger for you as I spend time with you today…

READ LUKE 22:1-46.

REFLECT

In his famous painting titled *The Sacrament of the Last Supper,* Salvador Dali envisioned the Upper Room as a spotless, surrealistic, almost otherworldly setting. But when we look carefully at this passage in Luke, we see that the reality was more down-to-earth: a borrowed room, a dinner cooked by men, lots of arguing around the table, and one person with a dark secret.

Why did Jesus bother with this awkward party? Why not just excuse himself from the bickering for an early bedtime? The answer can be found in a single word: "fulfillment" (22:16). Everything that the Law and the sacrifices had symbolized, everything that the prophets had predicted, everything that we've read in the Old Testament pointed to what was about to happen. Jesus was there to fulfill the mission given to him by his Father—to die on the cross for the sins of the world.

That's the message he wanted to symbolize for his followers with this meal. The bread helps us remember his body (22:19) and the fact that he took the punishment for our sin. The wine helps us remember his blood

(22:20) and the fact that he made the final sacrifice for the forgiveness of sin. This special meal represented a "new covenant," that is, a new agreement between God and humankind that would last forever.

In the midst of all this, Jesus singled out two people for special attention. Even though Judas was planning a betrayal, Jesus gave him several opportunities to change his mind (22:21-23; see also Matthew 26:20-25), all of which he ignored. And when Peter spoke up with characteristic bravado (22:33), Jesus set in motion the biggest lesson of Peter's life (22:34,54-62; see also John 21:15-19). At this special meal, when Jesus had the weight of the world on his shoulders (22:39-46), he still cared for individual people—including you and me. That's why he went to the cross.

APPLY

What do you think about when you take communion in your church or when you hear the word *communion?* Jesus said to remember him. What things do you remember about Jesus?

PRAY

Lord Jesus, I won't forget what you did for me through your body and blood. I'm so thankful that I can have a new and living relationship with you…

Reading 67

THE BIG DECISION

PRAY

Heavenly Father, open my mind and prepare my heart so that I may worship you in spirit and in truth...

READ JOHN 18.

REFLECT

Some people think Judas's motive in betraying Jesus was not hate or greed, but impatience. In their view, Judas had grown tired of waiting for Jesus to make a move, so he tried to force him to fight (18:1-3). "Use your power to set up a kingdom...now!" Whatever Judas's motive may have been, things spiraled out of control.

The trial that followed was the opposite of "due process." The religious leaders broke every rule of fairness because they had already made up their minds about the verdict (18:30-31). That's what happens when we let hate control us. If you have unresolved anger in your life, you'd be wise to get to the bottom of it before it damages your relationship with others and with God.

Pilate certainly didn't care about fairness; he just wanted to avoid hassle (18:29-35). It doesn't seem as though he cared too much about truth either (18:38). For many people today, a fuzzy notion of "tolerance" has replaced the reality of truth. "Whatever's true for you is fine. Whatever." Jesus cut through that kind of thinking with a clear statement, "Everyone on the side of truth listens to me" (18:37). Unless we stay connected to the Word of God, we'll wander further and further from the truth. That's why reading the Bible is so important.

Before he knew it, Pilate was faced with the most important decision of all time—what to do with Jesus? Sooner or later everyone must make that decision for himself or herself. Is Jesus a source of anger and frustration? Is he a hassle to be avoided? Or is he "the way and the truth and the life" (John 14:6). It's important to carefully ponder what you really think. It's the biggest decision you'll ever make.

APPLY

Do you believe there is such a thing as absolute truth? Why or why not? What decision have you made about Jesus?

PRAY

Lord Jesus, I want to be on the side of your truth. Help me grow in my ability to hear and my willingness to obey your voice...

Reading 68

PAID IN FULL!

PRAY

God, I begin this time with you by confessing my sins.... Thank you that you are willing and able to forgive and cleanse me...

READ JOHN 19.

REFLECT

John's account of the Crucifixion is like a well-written news article; it's full of detail. Yet he didn't sensationalize what happened. He just let the facts speak for themselves. It's hard to fully comprehend the torture Jesus endured—a flogging, thorns jammed into his scalp, punches in the face, nails through his hands and feet, a spear wound from point-blank range. It was a gruesome murder, but in those days crucifixion was common, so this one may not even have made the front page.

There's one angle to the story that comes through loud and clear: The religious leaders hated Jesus. Screaming for his execution, they were like wolves circling for the kill (19:6-16). It's a wonder no one asked them, "If it's true, as you say, that he's not the Son of God, why are you so worried about him?" It's a good question to ask anyone who vehemently opposes Jesus today. Finally, even Pilate realized what was driving the religious leaders, and in his own weak way, he said, "Enough!" (see 19:22).

But the significance of the Cross goes far beyond the historical facts. Just before he died Jesus shouted, "It is finished" (19:30). Some may have thought it was the final word of a beaten man. But in the Greek, the literal meaning of the word Jesus used was "paid in full." It was the same word that was stamped on a paid invoice. Instead of a dying gasp, Jesus' last words were a triumphant shout—"I've paid the price, the full price for all time for the sins of the world. Death no longer has the final say. The kingdom of darkness is defeated. I've completed my mission. It is finished!"

One interesting sidebar to John's "news article" is the story of Nicodemus (19:39). He didn't seem to respond to Jesus during their first encounter (John 3:1-21), but at the foot of the cross, the truth finally made sense, and this religious leader broke from his angry colleagues and publicly identified himself as a follower of Jesus. At the foot of the cross—that's where everything finally makes sense.

APPLY

Are you a "secret" disciple? If so, why? What is the significance of the Cross in your life?

PRAY

Lord Jesus, I thank you for all you endured on the cross for me. Today and every day I want to publicly identify myself as your follower...

Reading 69

THE LINCHPIN

PRAY

Heavenly Father, "I want to know Christ and the power of his resurrection" (Philippians 3:10). Open the eyes of my heart as I read your word today...

READ JOHN 20–21.

REFLECT

The resurrection of Jesus Christ is the linchpin of the Christian faith. If you eliminate that, as many have tried to do, everything comes apart. The apostle Paul acknowledged this when he said, "And if Christ has not been raised, our preaching is useless and so is your faith" (1 Corinthians 15:14). So it's important to understand the significance of the Resurrection, and that's what the people in our reading today are struggling to do.

Mary Magdalene was the first one to arrive at the tomb (20:1). Her love for Jesus was so deep that she was beyond the point of worrying who knew about it (20:10-17). Does that describe your love for Jesus? John had experienced the love of Jesus too (John 13:23), and he had responded by being a faithful follower. But deep down he was still confused (20:9). Do you ever feel that way? You've been a churchgoer for years, but something is missing. John had his conversion experience when he made a decision to believe in Jesus based on the evidence (20:8). Can you identify with John's need to find concrete evidence before being able to believe?

Thomas was walking the fine line between intellectual honesty and self-centered rejection, "Unless *I* see…*I* will not believe" (20:25, emphasis added). Sometimes our pride can prevent us from understanding more about God. Fortunately, Thomas didn't doubt forever (20:28). And on the beach Jesus gave Peter a new mission in life (21:15-19), even though he had denied Christ three times before Christ's death (Luke 22:54-62).

There's no getting around it. The resurrection of Jesus Christ is fundamental to the Christian faith. And when we experience the love and forgiveness of Jesus in the face of our own failures, we know that he is alive today.

APPLY

What is the most convincing evidence for the resurrection of Jesus Christ for you personally?

PRAY

My Lord and my God, I, too, marvel at the miracle of the empty tomb. Thank you for winning the battle over sin, death, and hell—for me…

Reading 70

SO LONG...FOR NOW!

PRAY

Lord, I want to know the reality of you in my life. I come into your presence eager to meet with you today...

READ ACTS 1:1-11.

REFLECT

Jesus went to great lengths to prove that he had risen from the dead (John 20:30-31; 21:25). He left a trail of evidence so that everyone, including you and me, would be able to understand what he had done on the cross and in the tomb. The odd thing is, the disciples *still* didn't get it; they were still looking for a political kingdom (1:6).

Sometimes it's hard to let go of our own ideas and let God work. It can be confusing and even painful, but until we give up our own plans, we can't experience God's. Jesus didn't have much time left on earth, so he didn't waste it correcting the disciples. What he did was communicate two important realities about his kingdom.

The first reality was *power.* The disciples would never be able to fulfill the mission Jesus was about to give them on their own (Matthew 28:18-20). They needed his presence and power—that's why he promised the Holy Spirit. Some people today overemphasize the Holy Spirit, almost making him more important than Jesus. Others seem to be afraid of the Holy Spirit, and they act as if he's not allowed to work anymore. The bottom line is that Jesus said we need the Holy Spirit's help, and we should be eager to ask for it.

The second reality was *witnessing*. The reason the disciples needed the Holy Spirit's power was to communicate a message (1:8). But Jesus told them to wait (1:4). Sometimes waiting for the Holy Spirit to create an opportunity for ministry is difficult. But real results come when we prayerfully wait for a sense of what the Holy Spirit wants us to do.

We can only imagine what Jesus' ascension to heaven looked like. No doubt it left an unforgettable impression on the disciples and confirmed everything Jesus had taught them. And the wonderful thing is, someday we won't have to use our imaginations. We'll be able to see Jesus for ourselves (1:11).

APPLY

What does it mean for a Christian to live with the end in mind?

PRAY

Jesus, your name is above all others. I bow my knees and confess that you are my Lord forever (Philippians 2:9-11). I look forward to the day when I will see you face to face... *

---

* Now turn to the Review Journal beginning on page 253 to record your key insights from the last five readings.

The Church Is Born

No matter where you go in the world today, you can find some kind of church to worship in. The question is—especially in Western countries—will you find any people in those churches? How did the church get its start? And what is it supposed to do?

Our next five readings take us back to the very beginnings of the church and help us understand its origins and purpose. Our last readings on the cross of Christ left the disciples reeling from the whirlwind of Jesus' death, resurrection, and ascension. They had no idea what would happen next. All Jesus said before he returned to heaven was "Wait" (Acts 1:4). *Wait*—wait for what?

As it turned out, Jesus was preparing to send them an incredible gift: the Holy Spirit who was "poured out" on all people on the Day of Pentecost. That event empowered Jesus' followers and ignited an evangelism explosion. It was the birth of the church.

So what is the church? Some people think the church is a particular denomination or a building. Some act as if the church is a social club for good people. The church may include these elements, but its essence is far more profound. The church is literally a union of Jesus and all those who have decided to follow him.

The mission of the church is to share the Good News of salvation with all people. This wasn't so clear at first. Since God had developed a special relationship with the Jewish people, many thought salvation was only for them. But God stepped in at Pentecost (Acts 2) and blew the doors wide open, making both the gospel and the church available to anyone who believes in Jesus Christ.

Once Jesus' followers got that straight, the church began to grow, increasing by thousands of people each day. It was out-of-control growth, and not even opposition or persecution could stop it. In fact, those things only accelerated its growth.

Why are so many churches nearly empty today? Perhaps it's because believers have lost sight of the original mission of the church. So your challenge as you dig into the next five readings is to rediscover what that mission is.

Reading 71

A SURPRISE GIFT

PRAY

Lord Jesus, thank you for promising to send your Holy Spirit. I'm waiting and open for whatever you want to show me...

READ ACTS 2.

REFLECT

How would you feel if you were one of the disciples at this point? For three years you've been at the center of the biggest story in the world. You heard Jesus preach and saw his miracles. You watched his crucifixion and witnessed his resurrection and ascension. But how do you feel now that it's all over? And what do you think is going to happen next?

The disciples couldn't answer those questions, so they returned to a familiar routine (2:1), gathering to worship on the Day of Pentecost—a Jewish harvest feast. That's a good thing to do after a big crisis—get together with other believers and worship God. Sometimes the only way to make sense of the things that happen in our lives is to wait in the presence of God.

In this case, the disciples' waiting led to an incredible spiritual breakthrough, the unleashing of the Holy Spirit (2:2-4). Because the Holy Spirit is part of the Trinity (Father, Son, and Holy Spirit), he has been present and active since the beginning of time (Genesis 1:2). But at Pentecost he was "poured out" on all who believed in Jesus (2:17-21), not just on a select few. And when the Holy Spirit enters your life, you'll never be the same again.

Peter was the first example of how the Holy Spirit completely changes a person. Peter had always been a "ready, fire, then aim" kind of guy, and that had gotten him into trouble more than once. But the Holy Spirit changed Peter from an impulsive deserter to a persuasive leader in the newly born church. Note how the Holy Spirit did it. He gave Peter insight into God's Word, a keen understanding of God's plan, uncommon courage and power, plus a supernatural effectiveness in ministry (2:40-41). Those are the traits of a person who has been filled with the Holy Spirit.

APPLY

What do you believe about the Holy Spirit? How have you experienced the presence and work of the Holy Spirit in your life?

PRAY

Come Holy Spirit, fill me with your insight and power so that I can become an effective witness to the reality of Jesus Christ...

Reading 72

A COMPLETELY DIFFERENT TEAM

PRAY

Heavenly Father, I want to leave my past behind and move forward with you. I'm ready for you to use me any way you see fit....

READ ACTS 3–4.

REFLECT

Have you ever watched a sporting event, say a basketball or football game, where the underdog team gets pummeled in the first half only to come back and win the game in the second half? That's what it's like for the disciples in our passage today. The "defeat" of the Cross is behind them, and the Holy Spirit has molded them into a completely different team that was destined to change the course of history.

It would have been natural for Peter to think, *Jesus got to be the front man all these years, while I did the following. Now it's my turn to get the spotlight.* But Peter still remembered the "halftime" speech Jesus had given years earlier (Luke 9:1-6), and he wasted no time putting it into action. Empowered by the Holy Spirit, Peter healed a lame man and preached another powerful sermon. And he did so with a Jesus-focused humility (3:6,11-26) that even the religious leaders recognized (4:13). That's what happens when we let the Holy Spirit empower us to share the Good News.

But not everyone was happy about the disciples' dramatic comeback (4:1-7). The fact is, when God begins to work, there will be opposition. You can expect it in your life and in your church. But opposition can't stop the church; in fact, that's what makes it grow (4:23-35), as communist governments in recent times have discovered. What stops the church dead in her tracks is when Christians don't focus on Jesus, don't witness for their faith, and don't rely on the power of the Holy Spirit.

Some think that the unique thing about the early church was its approach to money and possessions (4:32-37). It was impressive and challenges our commitment to giving today. But it seems that the church's willingness to practice "radical sharing" was the result of an even more impressive trait: unity (4:32). Imagine what we in the church could do today if we were "one in heart and mind."

APPLY

Would you say the church today is "one in heart and mind"? Why or why not? What could you do to encourage unity in your church?

PRAY

Lord, enable me "to speak your word with great boldness...and perform miraculous signs and wonders through the name of your holy servant Jesus" (4:29-30).

Reading 73

SEEDS IN THE WIND

PRAY

Lord Jesus, as I begin my time with you today, I want to confess my sins and ask for your forgiveness. Also bring to mind any people I need to forgive…

READ ACTS 6:8–8:8.

REFLECT

Stephen was a great leader in the early church (6:5,8), but he broke all the rules for guest preachers. His sermon was well beyond twenty minutes, his text was way too long (he tried to explain the entire Bible), and he finished with some high-volume, personal accusations. You'll never get a return invitation with that kind of message.

There was only one catch. God had given Stephen that message for the religious leaders, and tragically, they weren't in the least bit interested. For one thing, they were too angry. Sometimes people use anger to hide an inner struggle with God. If you find yourself getting angry a lot, it might be worth asking yourself, Is there something God is saying to me that I'm afraid to hear?

The other reason the leaders weren't open to Stephen's message was because they loved their religion more than they loved God (6:13-14). There's nothing wrong with appreciating your church and its traditions, but watch out if these things become too important to you. It has been said many times, and it's still true: Jesus never came to start a religion; he came to start a relationship—with you.

Stephen became the church's first martyr. His stoning was a horrible expression of hate (7:54-60). Yet God had a purpose for even this brutal act: to spread the message of salvation even further (8:4). The persecution unleashed that day was like a tornado in a field of dandelions; it spread the seeds everywhere (8:1-4). It also raised up a young man who would feature prominently in the remainder of the New Testament (8:1,3). Although it would take some time and a dramatic encounter with Jesus, the angry Saul would become the apostle Paul, a man destined to become the greatest evangelist of the early church. We should never doubt the power of God to change a life.

APPLY

Have you ever been persecuted for your faith? What brought it on? How did you react? What does the absence of persecution indicate?

PRAY

Lord, I want to boldly stand up for you, even though I sometimes feel hesitant. Please give me the courage to seize the moment for you...

Reading 74

UNSUNG HERO

PRAY

Lord God, I thank you for your Word, the Bible. Please help me both to understand and to apply what I learn from it today...

READ ACTS 8:26-40.

REFLECT

Philip wasn't one of the marquee attractions in the early church. Compared to big name apostles such as Peter or Paul, he seemed like a background player. Maybe that's how you feel at times. But the success of the church is not dependent on celebrities. It's dependent on ordinary people who are empowered by the Holy Spirit to become extraordinary witnesses for Jesus Christ.

That's what we see in this passage. Philip was just minding his own business when an angel (8:26) and the Spirit (8:29) orchestrated an opportunity for him to share the Good News. We must never lose sight of the fact that God is already at work in the world. Our job is to be sensitive to what he's doing and to be willing to let him use us at the right time.

So what can we learn about effectively sharing our faith from Philip's example? First, he started with questions (8:30), not answers. It's important to understand a person's struggle before we offer a solution. Next, Philip took time to explain what the Bible said about Jesus (8:35). One of the best contexts for that is a group Bible study. It's no wonder that one characteristic of growing churches today is an emphasis on small-group Bible studies.

But the most significant thing about Philip's example is that he was willing to take action even when he didn't know the *why.* Philip had no idea what he'd find as he headed for the desert (8:26). He only knew God wanted him to go down that road and be ready. That's the most important quality for anyone who wants to share the Good News or, for that matter, accomplish anything of value for God: a willingness to listen and obey no matter what. Is God nudging you to do something that doesn't fully make sense?

APPLY

How do you feel about sharing your faith with others? How might God be at work in the lives of your unbelieving friends? How could you have a part in what God is doing?

PRAY

Heavenly Father, I know you are at work all around me. Please open my eyes to what you are doing and give me the courage to respond to your prompting...

Reading 75

THE RAINBOW COALITION

PRAY

Heavenly Father, I'm so grateful for the ways you've opened my eyes to the truth about your Son, Jesus Christ. Show me more about him today...

READ ACTS 10:1–11:18.

REFLECT

We've come to a major turning point in our journey through the Big Story of the Bible. As we've seen, God's plan of salvation began with Abraham (Genesis 12:1-9) and was primarily linked to the history of the Jewish people. Now the circle widens to include "even" non-Jews as well (11:18). It might seem odd that this one story got so much ink in the book of Acts, but that only shows what a barrier there was between Jews and Gentiles in those days. To them, this was a really big deal.

Today's passage also emphasizes the active intervention of God in human events (10:3,17,19). Some people think of God as a clockmaker and the world as his clock; he made it, wound it up, and then had nothing more to do with it. But the Bible teaches that God not only created the world but also takes a hands-on approach to what happens in it. At key points, like in this passage, God steps in to guide events according to his loving plan. He does the same in the lives of individual people. Perhaps the best way to see the pattern is to look back on the events of your life.

But the overriding result of this meeting between Peter and Cornelius was to clarify a fundamental truth about God's Good News: Salvation through Jesus Christ is for everyone, not just a select group of insiders. The kingdom of heaven is the ultimate "rainbow coalition." That's not to say entrance is automatic. But it's open to all who believe in Jesus Christ (10:43) and therefore have received the Holy Spirit (10:47). Our challenge today is to keep the church as inclusive as God intended it to be.

APPLY

Are there people in your world who seem outside the reach of the gospel? What could you do to build a bridge between them and the Good News?

PRAY

Forgive me, Lord, for the times when I keep your Good News to myself. I'm ready and willing to talk about it with anyone you want me to... *

* Now turn to the Review Journal beginning on page 253 to record your key insights from the last five readings.

The Travels of Paul

As we discovered in our last set of readings, the book of Acts tells the story of how the Good News spread around the world after Jesus ascended into heaven. It's one of the fastest-paced, most exciting books in the Bible. (Even though our readings cover the highlights, you may want to read the whole book. It'll be well worth it.)

The key player in Acts is the apostle Paul, who described himself as "the least of the apostles" (1 Corinthians 15:9). His Jewish name was Saul, and he was one of the "young guns" among the Pharisees, a very traditional and devout group of Jewish leaders. At the same time, he was a Roman citizen by birth (Paul was his Roman name), which gave him a considerable amount of freedom and privilege in society at the time. As you will see, God dramatically intervened in Paul's life and used these two aspects of his background to make him the most effective missionary the world has ever known.

Our next five readings will follow Paul on his missionary journeys. Many Bibles have maps in the back that trace these journeys. Take a minute to check them out. You'll see that Paul covered a lot of ground, mostly on foot. He also had to endure all kinds of trouble. Listen to how Paul described the things he went through:

> I have worked much harder, been in prison more frequently, been flogged more severely, and been exposed to death again and again. Five times I received from the Jews the forty lashes minus one. Three times I was beaten with rods, once I was stoned, three times I was shipwrecked, I spent a night and a day in the open sea, I have been constantly on the move. I have been in danger from rivers, in danger from bandits, in danger from my own countrymen, in danger from

> Gentiles; in danger in the city, in danger in the country, in danger at sea; and in danger from false brothers. I have labored and toiled and have often gone without sleep; I have known hunger and thirst and have often gone without food; I have been cold and naked. Besides everything else, I face daily the pressure of my concern for all the churches. (2 Corinthians 11:23-28)

Why did Paul endure all that? It was for two reasons. First, Paul had a real encounter with Jesus on the Damascus road, and he realized right away that if Jesus Christ was alive, that was the only thing that really mattered. But second, Paul was God's "chosen instrument" to share the gospel with the Gentiles (Acts 9:15) and plant the church throughout the known world.

The great American evangelist Dwight L. Moody once said, "The world has yet to see what God could do with one man wholly dedicated to himself." That may be true. But if anyone has come close, it was the apostle Paul, as you are about to see.

Reading 76

THE ONLY QUESTION THAT MATTERS

PRAY

Lord, I believe your Word is "living and active," and I am ready to receive it into my soul and spirit today (Hebrews 4:12).

READ ACTS 9:1-31.

REFLECT

This passage describes one of the most dramatic life-change stories in the entire Bible. Literally in a flash (9:3), Saul went from "breathing out murderous threats against the Lord's disciples" (9:1) to "proving that Jesus is the Christ" (9:22). How could a person make such a complete turnaround?

The main reason was that God chose him (9:15). Just as God called Abraham centuries earlier (Genesis 12:1-3), he now tapped Saul for a special assignment. It reminds us that no one is outside of God's reach. He can use the most unlikely people for his glory. It also reminds us to be ready for God's call. He may have a special assignment for you.

A second reason was that Saul had an encounter with Jesus (9:3-6). It's sad, but people can spend a lifetime being involved in religious activities, yet never understanding the truth about Jesus. But on that dusty road, Saul finally got the point: If Jesus is alive, everything changes. The Good News has a way of forcing a person's hand. Once you understand who Jesus is (9:5), it changes your assumptions, your direction, your friends, your goals; it changes your life forever. As you will see, Saul was transformed into the apostle Paul and spent the rest of his life building the church.

Another reason for Saul's turnaround was the help of other believers. Ananias had the courage to accept him (9:17), and Barnabas had the wisdom to help him grow in his faith (9:27). Too often, Christians are judgmental about new believers and their "rough edges," but that only leaves new believers vulnerable to falling away.

Perhaps the final reason for Saul's turnaround was his willingness to respond to Jesus. When Saul was knocked off his horse, he asked, "Lord, what do You want me to do?" (9:6, NKJV). Once we understand the truth about Jesus, that's the only question that matters.

APPLY

How has Jesus changed your life? What special assignment might he be calling you to now?

PRAY

Lord Jesus, I'm overwhelmed by the knowledge that you want to have a personal relationship with me. If you have a special assignment for me today, I'm ready…

Reading 77

THE "P" WORD

PRAY

Lord God, I am eager for a closer walk with you. Show me how I can take another step toward you as I reflect on your Word today...

READ ACTS 13–14.

REFLECT

For many years I was involved in a prison ministry. We organized evangelistic events and Bible studies for inmates. Sometimes this made the wardens nervous. "You can have services for those who are already Christian," they'd tell us, "but we don't allow *proselytizing*." That's the big offense in our modern world. But as we see in our reading today, God commissioned Barnabas and Saul to do just that (13:2; also see Matthew 28:18-20). You can call it whatever you want, but sharing the Good News with others is the mission of the church.

Even so, that doesn't give us the right to jam the gospel down a person's throat. Notice the diplomacy Paul used throughout his message (13:16-43). He didn't back away from the hard truths of the gospel, but he presented them in a way that was respectful of his mixed audience (13:26) and that emphasized the positive (13:32,38-39). That approach gets results (13:42-44).

It also stirs up trouble. Throughout this exciting missionary journey, we see a combination of incredible results and vicious opposition. Paul and

Barnabas were stealing "market share" from these religious leaders, and they were jealous (13:45). But there was a deeper reason for the opposition (14:2). Becoming a Christian doesn't make a person close-minded; refusing to look at the truth does.

But there were two other factors that made Paul such an effective witness. The first was courage (14:19-20). You may never have to face an angry mob because of your faith, but you probably will have to take some risks. And when you do, not only will others hear the Good News, but you'll also gain a deeper relationship with God. The second factor was accountability. Paul was sent out by the church (13:1-3), and he reported back to them (14:26-28). The purpose of evangelism is to build Christ's church, not our reputations.

APPLY

What risk is God asking you to take in order to share the Good News with others?

PRAY

Lord, I don't feel like a very good "missionary," but I'm willing to share the Good News with others. Please give me the courage to take a risk for you today...

Reading 78

WHO IS THE CHURCH FOR?

PRAY

Heavenly Father, I'm so thankful that you have welcomed me into your presence through the death and resurrection of Jesus Christ...

READ ACTS 15.

REFLECT

Early in his career, pastor and writer Bill Hybels was forced to quit his position as youth pastor because the elders of his church felt he was attracting "the wrong kind of kids" to the youth group. Frustrated, Hybels started Willow Creek Community Church, which he intentionally designed to attract non-believers. It is now one of the largest churches in America.

Our passage today raises the same question that Bill Hybels wrestled with as a youth pastor: Who is the church for? In the first century, many thought the church was for the Jewish people (15:1), or at least for those who adopted Jewish customs. But the early Christians needed to understand that the key to God's plan of salvation wasn't race; it was grace (15:11). Of course, the church is a place for Christians to grow in their faith. But if it ever stops attracting "the wrong kind of people," it has lost touch with God's vision.

Another fascinating angle to this passage is how the early church handled a divisive issue. Notice that when the disagreement became public (15:2), the opponents didn't revert to gossip or infighting. Instead, they came together (15:2-4), listened to all sides (15:5-18), remained sensitive to the work of the Holy Spirit (15:8), and finally accepted the decision of the leader (15:19). It's a model the church today would do well to follow.

The chapter ends with a sad but realistic postscript. After risking their lives together for the gospel and avoiding a major split in the emerging church, Paul and Barnabas couldn't agree on a personnel issue, so they parted company (15:37-40; see also Acts 13:13). Disagreements among Christians happen, and when they do, we should seek God's wisdom and the counsel of others to avoid unnecessary division. But even when that isn't possible, God can bring good out of our failings. In this case, the disagreement doubled the missionary effort (15:39-41).

APPLY

What kinds of people does your church attract? Why do you think this is the case? Do you have a disagreement with another group of Christians? What instruction does this passage offer you?

PRAY

Holy Spirit, I ask for your guidance to know when I should stand up for what I believe and when I should compromise to avoid division...

Reading 79

KNOWING GOD'S WILL

PRAY

Thank you, Lord, for the example of Paul. May I be as abandoned to you as he was...

READ ACTS 16–20.

REFLECT

Will God punish me if I don't figure out his will? What if I try but get it wrong? Maybe you've felt like that prior to a big decision in your life. No doubt Paul was searching for God's direction at the beginning of this new missionary journey. How can we know God's will?

The starting point is waiting on the Lord (Acts 13:2-3). It's natural to chart our own course and then ask God to bless it. But that can get us into trouble. It's far better to pray, fast, seek advice, and wait for the Holy Spirit to guide us. That doesn't mean we need to be paralyzed. Notice that Paul seemed to misunderstand God's will at first. He tried to go to Asia, then to Bythinia, and both times God stopped him (16:6-7). Finally, God opened the door to Macedonia (16:9-10). When we have taken time to earnestly seek God's will, we can step out in faith, even if the way still seems unclear. God can use our detours to get us where he wants us.

But the road won't always be easy. Make a quick list of the number of bad things that happened to Paul and his companions in each of these cities.

("Lord, I thought *you* told me to go to Macedonia.") The curious thing is that God's work often does not look successful. That's because he uses our weaknesses to accomplish his purposes (2 Corinthians 12:9-10). But no matter what happened, good or bad, Paul stayed focused on the right motivation for ministry (20:24), and so should we.

He also used different strategies, depending on whom he was trying to reach. To those who were familiar with the Bible, he "reasoned with them from the Scriptures" (17:2). But to those who weren't familiar with the Law and the Prophets, he used art and culture to build bridges for sharing the Good News (17:18-23; 18:1-11). That's an important example for anyone trying to communicate the gospel in a postmodern world.

APPLY

How do you seek God's will? Has God ever used a detour in your life to accomplish his agenda for you or others?

PRAY

Heavenly Father, when I look back on my life, I can see how you've been guiding me all along. If there is a new direction you want me to take, I ask that you give me the courage to step out in faith…

Reading 80

AHOY MATES!

PRAY

Lord, the most important part of my day is spending this time with you. You have the full attention of my mind, my heart, and my emotions…

READ ACTS 25–28.

REFLECT

What a great story! There are conflicting passions, secret plots, political tensions, a dramatic shipwreck, plus an ending that sets the stage for a sequel. Sounds like a thriller, and it is. The book of Acts is one of the "best reads" in the Bible.

On the surface it seemed as if events were out of control, that Paul's last-ditch appeal to Caesar (25:11) had shipwrecked his ministry. But underneath the apparent disaster, God had a plan, like a strong current beneath the choppy waters. He wanted Paul to preach the gospel in the world's most powerful city, and he gets him there courtesy of the Roman authorities. If you are experiencing some kind of disaster right now, you may want to ask God to open your eyes to his underlying agenda—"Lord, what are you trying to say to me through this difficult situation?"

In the midst of seeming chaos, there are two things that kept Paul going. The first was his single-minded focus on the mission God had given him (Acts 9:15). Even under the pressure of the confrontation with King Agrippa,

Paul never blinked (26:20,28-29). He didn't care if people thought he was crazy. All he cared about was sharing the Good News. You, too, can become an incredibly powerful witness when you stop worrying about what people will think about you. The second thing that kept Paul going was the intervention of the Holy Spirit. Several times along the way, God miraculously intervened in events (27:23-24,44; 28:1-10). When you find yourself in a situation where the only way forward is to boldly trust God, you'll begin to experience more of the Holy Spirit's power in your life.

In the end, it seemed that the result of Paul's ministry was inconclusive. But the truth is, he accomplished exactly what God wanted him to: to preach the gospel to the Gentiles and the Jews and to plant the church of Jesus Christ in the major cities of the known world. Well done, good and faithful servant!

APPLY

What mission has God given you? What would it mean for you to boldly trust him in this situation?

PRAY

Lord, Paul is an inspiration. I'm ready to accept any mission you want to give me, and I ask for the Holy Spirit's help to accomplish it… *

---

* Now turn to the Review Journal beginning on page 253 to record your key insights from the last five readings.

Paul to the Churches

As we discovered in our studies through the book of Acts, Paul traveled all over the Roman Empire preaching the gospel and starting churches. It was an exciting and dangerous mission, and in spite of all the difficulties he encountered, he was effective. Paul planted churches in many of the major cities of the known world.

But his church-planting success created a problem. How could he keep these communities of new believers going in the right direction after he was gone? Most of them were living in pagan cities filled with idolatry and immorality. Often, Paul only had time to preach the very basics of the Good News before his enemies ran him out of town. There was so much more he needed to communicate about the gospel, Christian living, the church, and so on.

In addition to his enemies, Paul had to contend with false teachers who were roaming around confusing people by trying to discredit him and his ministry. And on top of all this, Paul was put in prison, so he couldn't do anything even if he wanted to. It must have been incredibly frustrating and worrisome to see his lifework eroding before his very eyes. But that's why he was such a passionate letter writer. It was his primary strategy—in addition to prayer—for strengthening and building the church.

In our next readings we'll cover portions from Paul's letters to churches in five different cities—Rome, Galatia, Ephesus, Philippi, and Colosse. In each letter there are different features, depending on the different needs that existed. But there are also some similarities, such as what the gospel was all about. That never changed.

As you read Paul's letters, you may want to ask yourself, What could I do to strengthen and encourage the Christians around me? In some ways the circumstances Paul was addressing were very different from today. But in other ways they are surprisingly similar. As you read the next section, ask God to show you how you can join Paul in his mission to build the church.

Reading 81

AMEN, BROTHER!

PRAY

Heavenly Father, thank you for sending your Son to die for me and your Holy Spirit to live in me. I want these facts to be the most important influences in my life...

READ ROMANS 8.

REFLECT

This chapter reminds me of the sermons of Dr. Martin Luther King Jr. It starts slow and methodically, but as it builds a case, it gradually picks up steam, and by the end, Paul has us on our feet shouting, "Amen!" For a creative way to understand this passage, try reading it aloud, imagining you are preaching to a large crowd.

Paul began his "sermon" at the bottom line of the gospel: Jesus Christ overcame sin and death and then gave us a new Spirit (8:1-4). But it's not good enough just to understand the gospel; we must allow it to affect our actions. And Paul reminds us that there is no middle ground; either we are controlled by our sinful nature or we are controlled by the Holy Spirit (8:5-17).

Making that choice isn't always easy. Life is complicated, and many situations are ambiguous. But the Holy Spirit can guide us through, even when we don't know what to pray. I sometimes apply verse 26 literally. When I'm overwhelmed, I'll pray, *Holy Spirit, I don't know what the answer is, but would you intercede for…,* and then I identify the situation or perhaps repeat a person's name several times and wait in stillness. Often I sense God's power more so than if I came up with a "solution" to tell God about.

Romans 8:28 is one of those Bible verses we all should memorize. Note that it doesn't say everything in your life will be good, fun, or successful. That wasn't Paul's experience (8:18). But God will use everything, even bad things, for your ultimate good if you belong to him. Being a Christian won't make your life easy, but it will give you the assurance that God really loves you and that he is in charge of your life. That's what makes you more than a conqueror (8:37).

APPLY

What are the controlling influences in your life? What would it mean for you to be controlled by the Spirit?

PRAY

Holy Spirit, there are so many situations in my life and in this world that I have no answer for. But I know you are in charge. So here are a few things I ask you to pray about for me…

Reading 82

TWO LISTS

PRAY

Lord God, your Word is such an incredible gift. Where else can I go to find out what you are like and how you want me to live? Please help me hear what you want to say to me today…

READ GALATIANS 5:16–6:10.

REFLECT

Today people are uncomfortable with absolute truth, the idea that some things are always right and other things are always wrong. For them, truth is more like a personal preference—"What's true for you may not be true for me."

That wasn't Paul's worldview. For him there was a sharp contrast between right and wrong, between good and evil, as we see in this passage. He began with a clear picture of the sinful nature (5:19-21). Don't skip over the list too fast. Although it contains some sins we're usually careful to avoid (such as idolatry and witchcraft), it also contains others that may hit closer to home (such as jealousy, envy, and selfish ambition). Ironically, the list sounds like a plot summary of many current movies and television programs. But Paul's message is that the sinful nature is no joke, and it has serious consequences (5:21).

In contrast, Paul offered a second list, which he called the "fruit of the Spirit" (5:22-23). These are the traits we should cultivate in our lives. It takes work and time, but faithful effort to grow in godliness eventually pays off. This list also gives us a way to think about God's will when we have a choice between two seemingly worthy options. In such cases, ask yourself, Which option is most likely to help me develop more fruit of the Spirit? That's a good direction to go.

But removing the "weeds" and cultivating the "fruit" in our lives is tough work, so Paul suggests two sources of help. The first is fellow believers (6:1-5). Even when we know the difference between right and wrong, we still mess up. That's when we need Christian friends who can help restore the broken parts of our lives. The second is the Holy Spirit. Some people are hesitant about the Holy Spirit. Not Paul. He tells us to "live by the Spirit" (5:16), to be "led by the Spirit" (5:18), and to "keep in step with the Spirit" (5:25). The Holy Spirit is God's help for us today.

Apply

What are some weeds you'd like to remove from your life? What fruit would you like to cultivate in your life?

Pray

Holy Spirit, I want to live for you, I want to be led by you, and I want to keep in step with you throughout this day—and always…

Reading 83

THE FIGHT OF YOUR LIFE

PRAY

Lord, I praise you for who you are, and I thank you for what you've done in my life. Open my eyes to what you want to teach me today…

READ EPHESIANS 6:10-20.

REFLECT

Why do people "celebrate" Halloween? In a society that is eliminating religious symbols from public places, why do we spend a full month displaying antireligious symbols such as witches, goblins, and devils? What's so good about evil?

"Absolutely nothing!" is what the apostle Paul would say. And before we can understand what he had in mind when he described the "armor of God," we have to come to grips with why we need it in the first place. Life on earth is a spiritual battle. The devil is real, he opposes God, and he is scheming against God's children (6:11-12). It's worth reflecting for a minute on the nature of those schemes. Sometimes they take the form of things that are obviously evil, such as the occult, substance abuse, or promiscuity. At other times they are subtle, such as pride, greed, or envy. Either way, the devil uses them to destroy what God wants to do in our lives.

That's why we need protection. The way we get protection is to use God's armor, such as truth, righteousness, the gospel, faith, salvation, God's Word, and prayer (6:14-18). Those aren't just nice words for church people. They are the weapons God has given us to survive in the spiritual battle.

Notice that Paul encouraged his readers to be proactive. "Be strong... stand your ground...stand firm...be alert...pray in the Spirit." No matter who you are, no matter how long you've been a Christian, you can expect the devil's schemes. The apostle Peter was even more direct. He said that Satan was like a lion looking for someone to devour (1 Peter 5:8). This passage reminds us that the best defense against evil is a good offense. Put on the full armor of God.

Apply

What has made you aware that you are in a spiritual battle? What are you doing to put on God's armor?

Pray

Lord, I'm not afraid, because I know you have already won the battle and I belong to you. But I don't want to become complacent, so I ask you to help me put on your armor for whatever battle you call me to...

Reading 84

GIVE PEACE A CHANCE

PRAY

Heavenly Father, my life is so stressful and discouraging at times. I would love to experience more of your peace and joy today...

READ PHILIPPIANS 4:2-9.

REFLECT

It's interesting that Paul wrote this famous passage about God's peace at a time when he was in prison (Philippians 1:12-14,17) and there was interpersonal tension in the church (4:2-3). We can experience peace not only when everything is smooth but also in the midst of the problems of life. So how exactly does Paul say that we can do this? It requires at least three conscious decisions.

First is the decision to rejoice whether we feel like it or not (4:4). That's because the focus of our rejoicing is the Lord, not our circumstances. We praise God for who he is, not for what may be happening to us at the moment. I once attended a meeting where several Christians gathered to discuss some very stressful issues that threatened to divide the group. I noticed one of my friends seemed especially happy. When I asked why, he said that during the break, he had walked around the perimeter of the parking lot in the dark, praising the Lord. He was rejoicing in the midst of the tension.

The second decision is to pray (4:6). Sometimes we become so overwhelmed by our worries that we can't sleep. If you find yourself lying in bed, imagining worst-case scenarios for your life, get up and pray. I find it helpful to get on my knees and pour out my worries to God. Then, while still on my knees, I raise my hands as high as I can and praise the Lord. I've found that these middle-of-the-night "prayer meetings" are the times when I most experience the peace that "transcends all understanding." And I'm usually able to go right back to sleep too.

The third decision is to focus on positive things (4:8). Sometimes we have so many problems that they "fill the screen" of our minds. That's when we need to click the "minimize" button on our worries and open some new screens that remind us of God's goodness. Rejoice, pray, minimize. That's the way to exchange anxiety for peace.

APPLY

Make a list of the things that are worrying you today. Then make a list of the things for which you can praise God.

PRAY

Lord, I give my worries and anxieties to you, even though you already know what they are. And I rejoice because you have a plan for my life, and nothing can separate me from your love...

Reading 85

DRIFTING AWAY

PRAY

Lord God, fill me with the knowledge of your will that I may bear fruit and live a life that pleases you...

READ COLOSSIANS 1:1-23.

REFLECT

Sometimes we hear that a friend or acquaintance or a musical artist or other well-known person has become a Christian. Over time, though, the person's life seems to suggest that he or she has moved on to other beliefs. How can we encourage Christians who may be drifting away from their faith? That was the challenge the apostle Paul faced when he wrote this letter to the Colossians.

Paul started by emphasizing the positive (1:3-6). Growing in Christ doesn't always follow a straight line. Sometimes an initial commitment is followed by a detour. Instead of scolding the Colossians, Paul praised their good start and reminded them of their positive influence on others. He also assured them of his prayers (1:9-14). New believers need encouragement and prayer, not criticism.

But the Colossians *were* in danger of getting offtrack by adding things to the gospel. Some thought they had to follow Jewish rules to be a Christian. Others thought they had to obtain secret knowledge. Paul corrected these misunderstandings by going back to the heart of the gospel: Jesus Christ. He chose every phrase of his carefully worded statement (1:15-20) to communicate another important truth about Jesus. Now they were ready to hear the Good News, and Paul gave it to them in concentrated form (1:21-23).

Paul's strategy for helping the Colossians provides a good example for us. Too often we expect perfection of new believers and give up as soon as they fall—"See, I knew he wasn't genuine." But God knows what's in a person's heart, not us. We need to pray for people who may have drifted from the faith, that they would get refocused on Jesus Christ.

Apply

Do you know any "drifting Christians"? What could you do to encourage their faith this week? How could you help refocus them on Jesus Christ?

Pray

Lord Jesus, there is so much to know about you and so much to praise you for. Most of all, I thank you for reconciling me to God... *

---

* Now turn to the Review Journal beginning on page 253 to record your key insights from the last five readings.

PAUL TO THE LEADERS

According to J. Robert Clinton in his book *The Making of a Leader,* "Leadership is a dynamic process in which a man or woman with God-given capacity influences a specific group of God's people towards His purposes for the group." One of the most important tasks of a Christian leader is preparing and empowering new leaders. In fact, the best way for a Christian leader to have a lasting influence is to leave his or her ministry—whether it is a large organization or a small Sunday-school class—in capable hands.

After many years of preaching the gospel and planting churches, Paul's active ministry was nearing an end (2 Timothy 4:6-7). He realized that finding the next generation of leaders for the church was his final challenge. He even summarized his leadership development strategy in a letter to his protégé Timothy: "And the things you have heard me say in the presence of many witnesses entrust to reliable men who will also be qualified to teach others" (2 Timothy 2:2). For Paul, the future of the church was all about finding good people to lead it.

In our next five readings, we see Paul writing to train and encourage the leaders of the early church, primarily Timothy. He provided a job description for church leaders, warned against the pitfalls of leadership, clarified some key issues, and stressed the importance of two fundamentals of Christian leadership: the gospel and God's Word.

These readings also give us some insight into the stresses of the first-century church. For one thing, it was growing in spite of persecution. As we saw in the book of Acts, God sometimes uses persecution to expand his kingdom. But the church was also encountering internal strife because of false teachers. And of these two stresses, it is clear that Paul saw the latter as the more serious threat to the growth of the church. It still is. Paul confronted these twin challenges with a combination of encouragement and correction for leaders.

Maybe you don't think of yourself a leader, but as you reflect on the definition of Christian leadership above, you may want to reconsider. Everyone, including you, can influence others for God's purposes. If that's true, the apostle Paul has some good advice for all of us, as you are about to discover.

Reading 86

THE HABITS OF HIGHLY EFFECTIVE LEADERS

PRAY

Lord, I want to grow in my walk with you. I'm ready to be shaped by your Word today…

READ 1 TIMOTHY 3.

REFLECT

Success creates problems. That's what Paul was feeling when he wrote this letter to his protégé, Timothy. In spite of opposition and hardships, Paul's missionary journeys were incredibly successful. Churches were popping up all over the place. But the problem was, who was going to lead them?

Anyone who's been part of a growing organization knows that good leadership is essential. Jesus understood this and made hands-on leadership training one of his highest priorities (Luke 6:12-16; 9:1-6; 10:1-17). Now Paul faced the same challenge; if his church-planting success was to last beyond his lifetime, he had to find a new generation of leaders. The question was how?

Paul started with "job descriptions" that set high standards (3:2-13). And whether or not you think of yourself as a leader in your church, these are good goals to work on. Notice that the lists balance personal traits, family issues, and a good outside reputation. A Christian leader is a well-rounded person, not just a good preacher.

Today people sometimes get hung up on the details of "eldership." They act as if the elders are the most important part of the church. In assuming this, they lose sight of a more important principle. The church doesn't belong to its leaders; it belongs to God (3:15). He's the boss. Leaders serve him by serving others. Anyone who aspires to leadership in the church must add one more trait to the list: humility.

But the fact remains that if the church is going to grow, quality leadership is the biggest need. That doesn't mean you need to be the world's greatest preacher or church planter. The church needs solid leadership at every level—Sunday-school teachers, outreach program leaders, home-group leaders, and more. If that is so, perhaps you should begin developing your leadership qualities right away. God may be calling you soon.

Apply

What could you do to develop your leadership abilities? How could you begin to use these abilities in your church?

Pray

Lord, you know I'm still growing in many areas. But I'm willing to use the abilities you've given me in your church. If you call me to leadership, I'll follow…

Reading 87

SHOW ME THE MONEY

PRAY

Lord Jesus, you have offered me a pearl of great price (Matthew 13:45-46). I value my relationship with you more than anything else…

READ 1 TIMOTHY 6:3-21.

REFLECT

I once heard a prisoner describe the goal of his life before he went to jail: "All I wanted was some more of them dead presidents." We may not be as candid about our interest in money, but the truth is, it has a powerful influence in our lives. The apostle Paul knew this, so he made a special point in his letter to Timothy of explaining at least three important financial principles for Christians.

1. *Loving money leads to evil* (6:10). Having money isn't evil; loving it is. But what does it mean to "love" money? When we love someone, we think about that person all the time, make decisions with him or her in mind, devote a lot of our time to him or her. Does that describe your "relationship" with money? If it does, watch out.
2. *Greed leads to strife* (6:9-10). You can tell money has become too important when it infects other areas of our lives. In the early church the greed of some leaders weakened their commitment to sound teaching, which produced "envy, strife, malicious talk, evil

suspicions, and constant friction" (6:4-5). Even today, money is at the bottom of many church squabbles.

3. *Godliness leads to contentment* (6:6). Some people think that having lots of money will make them happy. But often it only makes them hungry for more. John D. Rockefeller, one of the richest men in the world, was once asked, "How much is enough?" He answered, "Just a little bit more." The secret of happiness is not to pursue more money; it is to pursue the goals and values of God's kingdom and then to let the chips fall where they may (Matthew 6:33).

But we should be careful not to conclude that just because money and possessions have a powerful influence, they are all bad. Paul acknowledged that some Christians will be rich (6:17). Still, he commanded them to make God their first priority by doing good deeds and sharing their resources. That's a challenge we in the Western church need to accept.

Apply

It is often said that you can tell a lot about a person by examining his or her checkbook. What does your checkbook say about you?

Pray

Lord, thank you for the ways you have blessed me with material things. Please help me to have more passion for serving you than for spending money…

Reading 88

YOU'VE GOT A FRIEND

PRAY

Lord, there are times in my life when I get tired and worn down, both physically and spiritually. Please renew my passion to know you and my desire to serve you as I read your Word today...

READ 2 TIMOTHY 2.

REFLECT

Mentoring has become a big deal these days. Researchers have found that mentoring makes a positive impact in the lives of troubled youth. It also helps employees to be more successful in their jobs.

In this passage we see Paul acting as a spiritual mentor to Timothy. Paul was keenly aware of Timothy's conversion and was instrumental in helping him discover his spiritual gift (2 Timothy 1:5-6). Now Paul is writing to coach Timothy on how to be an effective leader in the emerging church. If you find yourself eager for a spiritual mentor, try reading 1 and 2 Timothy as if Paul were writing just to you. Think of Paul as your spiritual mentor.

Paul used four images to help Timothy understand his ministry (2:3-7,15). The thing that a soldier, an athlete, a farmer, and a workman all have in common is their focus on the task. If they get distracted, they will fail to accomplish their objective. That was Paul's message to Timothy and to you: No matter how difficult things get, stay focused on the mission of sharing and living out the gospel. Take a minute to reflect further on each of Paul's examples (2:7). What else do you learn about living an effective Christian life?

It's interesting that although Paul mentioned several potential distractions, including the catch-all "evil desires of youth" (2:22), the one he seemed most concerned about was arguing (2:14-26). Some Christian leaders today seem more interested in arguing with one another about nonessential issues than in sharing the gospel with a needy world. If Paul were here today, he'd say, "Knock it off! You're getting distracted." Even Christian leaders need a mentor.

APPLY

Think of some people who are older and wiser in the faith and life experience than you are. Who do you think would make a good spiritual mentor for you? How could you approach this person to ask him or her about it?

PRAY

Lord God, forgive me for the ways I allow myself to become distracted. With your help, I want to be a focused and effective witness for you…

Reading 89

FINISHING WELL

PRAY

Lord God, I thank you for the gift of your Word. Help me to "pray it in and live it out" today...

READ 2 TIMOTHY 3:10–4:8.

REFLECT

Psychologists talk about "doorknob statements," that is, the last thing patients say as they linger at the door before leaving a counseling session. It usually is the main thing on their mind. This passage is like a long doorknob statement from Paul. He knows he's about to leave this world (4:6), and these verses are his parting thoughts to Timothy before he dies.

First, Paul emphasized suffering (3:12). Paul said suffering is inevitable, not just for evangelists and church planters, but for "everyone who wants to live a godly life." It's the one Bible promise you'll never find on a bookmark or poster. That doesn't mean we should go looking for trials and troubles, but we shouldn't be shocked when they come. In fact, God will use them to help us grow (James 1:2-4; 1 Peter 1:6-7).

Next, Paul emphasized Scripture (3:15-16). If Jesus Christ is the Cornerstone of the church (1 Peter 2:4-8), the Bible is the plumb line for keeping it in line with God's priorities and values (Amos 7:7-8). Paul stressed that the Bible is like no other book because it expresses the words of God ("God-breathed" in 3:16), and it therefore has at least three purposes: (1) *to explain* God's plan of salvation, (2) *to train* us for godly living, and (3) *to motivate* us for good works. Are those the outcomes of your Bible reading?

Finally, Paul challenged Timothy to continue his mission of preaching the word (4:1-2). It's interesting to read how Paul summed up his own experiences and mission in life (3:10-11). How would you sum up yours? In spite of all the things that happened to Paul along the way, he had the joy of knowing he was finishing well (4:7-8).

APPLY

How would you describe your mission for the rest of your life? What will it take for you to finish well?

PRAY

Heavenly Father, I want to commit the rest of my life to pursuing the goals that matter most to you. Help me finish well for your glory...

Reading 90

I Want to Be Ready

Pray

If you can, go outside or to a window and look up into the sky. Pray aloud, offering God thanksgiving and praise for what you are thankful for today.

Read 1 Thessalonians 4:13–5:11.

Reflect

One issue that caused confusion for leaders in the early church was the second coming of Christ. Most believers were aware that Jesus said he was coming back, but when? Some thought it would be in a matter of days, so they quit working. Others claimed he had already returned. The church needed some clear teaching on this slippery issue.

The same is true today. Occasionally we hear of a group of people who have sold all their goods and gone to a mountaintop to wait for the Second Coming. Or we hear of a Bible teacher who claims to have figured out exactly when Christ will return. No doubt, such people are motivated by an intense and admirable devotion to Christ. But they've lost sight of what the Bible says about the subject.

Paul didn't hesitate to talk about what Christ's return would be like. He said it will be a spectacular event (4:16-17). Just because some people misunderstand the Second Coming doesn't mean we should avoid the topic altogether. Jesus himself took time to explain to his followers what it will be like (4:15; see also Matthew 24:1-51). Our challenge today is to neither overemphasize nor underemphasize this important fact.

But Paul was hesitant to talk about *when* the Second Coming would happen (5:1-3). The main thing we need to know is that it will be a surprise, like a "thief in the night." Instead of trying to determine exactly when it will happen, we should focus on being alert and self-controlled (5:6-8) so that no matter when Jesus returns, we'll be ready.

If we can keep that balance, the hope of Christ's return should be one of the most encouraging realities of the Christian life (4:18). Imagine what it will be like to hear the trumpets and the voice of the archangel and then to finally see the Lord face to face.

APPLY

How does the reality of Christ's return affect the way you live your life? How should it?

PRAY

Lord Jesus, the fact that someday I'll be able to see you face to face boggles my mind and fills me with joy. Help me live this day with that wonderful truth in mind... *

---

* Now turn to the Review Journal beginning on page 253 to record your key insights from the last five readings.

The Apostles' Teaching

Our next five readings guide us through the writings of four great leaders of the first-century church. They form a mosaic of the apostles' teaching.

Although he was not originally one of the twelve disciples, Paul became a believer when he met Jesus on the Damascus road, as we discovered in an earlier section. After that, he became the greatest evangelist and most prolific writer in the entire New Testament. If you want to know what it means to go all out for the gospel, read the letters of Paul.

But in the Gospel accounts, Peter was the most prominent disciple. He frequently acted on impulse, which sometimes led to some incredible breakthroughs (Luke 9:20) and other times led to some humiliating failures (Luke 22:54-62). But Jesus restored him and gave him a new mission. The new Peter was the first one to explain the gospel on the Day of Pentecost and the first one to take it to the Gentiles. His lifetime of successes and failures as a follower of Jesus gave him deep insight into the Christian faith. If you want a clear and passionate expression of the implications of being born again, read the letters of Peter.

In the New Testament, five different people have the name James. But it was James the brother of Jesus (Matthew 13:55; Mark 6:3) who was the leader of the church in Jerusalem (Acts 15:13-21) and who later wrote the book of James. Perhaps because of his relationship to Jesus, or because of his wisdom, he was authoritative, straightforward, and direct. If you want to understand the practical implications of the faith, read the letter of James.

Of all the disciples, John had one of the closest relationships with Jesus (John 13:23). But it wasn't until John saw the empty tomb that he finally believed Jesus was who he said he was (John 20:8). At the beginning of his life, he was a rough-and-tumble sort of guy. But by the end of his life, he had become one of the most thoughtful of all the disciples. If you want to understand the deep implications of Jesus' love, read the letters of John.

So get ready to dig into the letters of the men who were closest to Jesus. They have a lot to say.

Reading 91

THE ACTIVE INGREDIENT

PRAY

Lord, so much of this world is devoted to chasing the illusion of love. But I pray that you would help me know and experience the reality of your love today...

READ 1 CORINTHIANS 13.

REFLECT

I married Carol Capra on June 4, 1977, and she has been one of the greatest blessings that God has brought into my life. But every once in a while, we get on each other's nerves. In fact, I am ashamed to admit that there have been times when our frustration with each other has lasted several days. When that happens, I've discovered the best thing to do is to get by myself and prayerfully read this chapter in 1 Corinthians. I've been amazed at how quickly these words can challenge and melt my hardened heart.

Paul had just finished an extended discussion of spiritual gifts, but he called love "the most excellent way" (1 Corinthians 12:31). That doesn't mean things like wisdom or faith or healing are bad (1 Corinthians 12:7-11). It's just that without love, even the most gifted person has missed the point. Love is the active ingredient of the Christian life.

At the heart of this chapter (13:4-7), Paul answered the question, What is love? You can read all the literature that's ever been written and not find a better expression of love than this. It's definitely worth memorizing. And yet, as wonderful as this passage is, it's still only the second-best expression of love ever. The best was Jesus Christ's death on the cross for the sins of the world.

When you think about it, we spend so much of our lives pursuing things that are temporary or just plain worthless. This passage reminds us that the things in life that have the greatest value are faith, hope, and love. But love is the greatest. And the best way to find it is to give it away.

APPLY

In what ways are you pursuing faith, hope, and love in your life? How could you live out Paul's definition of love this week?

PRAY

Thank you, Lord Jesus, for your incredible love for me. With your help, I intend to share that love with the people in my world through my words, attitudes, and actions...

Reading 92

SUPERNATURAL HERO

PRAY

Heavenly Father, show me just a little bit more today of what it means to live by faith and not by sight...

READ 2 CORINTHIANS 4:1–6:2.

REFLECT

Clark Kent is a mild-mannered newspaper reporter. But when evil and danger lurk, he steps out of sight and is transformed into...Superman! After that, the bad guys don't stand a chance. The comic-book hero gives us just a little picture of what Paul had in mind when he described what it means to be a "new creation" in Christ (5:17). When we hear and receive the gospel, everything in our life changes, and the devil doesn't stand a chance.

You'd think a message like that would be wildly popular. But the opposite was true, as we've discovered in our last few sections. So in this passage the apostle Paul described his efforts to share this unpopular message (4:2,8-12), and in so doing, he gave us some incredible insights into the meaning of the gospel.

The first thing he emphasized was "this ministry" (4:1), which he later described as a "ministry of reconciliation" (5:18). Ever since Adam and Eve sinned in the Garden of Eden, humankind has been separated from God. That's the Big Problem. But the Big Story is that Jesus died on the cross for the sins of the world. The Good News is that through faith in Jesus Christ we can be reunited with God.

No wonder Paul referred to the gospel as "this treasure" (4:7). Amazingly, God chose to place that message in "jars of clay," that is, in weak, faltering people like you, the apostle Paul, and me. Even so, as a new person you have a new mission, to be Christ's ambassador (5:20). That makes you a supernatural hero.

APPLY

In what ways have you become a new creation as a result of following Jesus? How would you act and speak if you were Christ's ambassador?

PRAY

Lord, forgive me for not feeling or acting like your ambassador. But I ask that you would enable me to share with others the treasure you've given me...

Reading 93

SURE, I'M SURE

PRAY

Lord Jesus, I rejoice because the hope you have offered me is more valuable and lasting than anything this world has to offer...

READ 1 PETER 1:1–2:12.

REFLECT

An agnostic is a person who says it isn't possible to know God. For some, this seems intellectually honest, but, in fact, it is a hopeless dilemma. The one thing agnostics believe is that it isn't possible to believe. That takes a lot of faith.

The apostle Peter was a fisherman, not an intellectual. But he was very, very sure about what he believed. The reason? He had seen the risen Christ (John 21:1-25). When you think about it, that's the only thing that could explain why a bunch of powerless, uneducated disciples could all of a sudden become fearless evangelists, willing to suffer and sacrifice their lives. If they knew the Resurrection wasn't true, they would have backed off. But they couldn't because they had seen Jesus alive again.

So what was Peter so sure about? The first thing was the "new birth" (1:3). Being free of our sin and reunited with God is like being born again (1:23; see also John 3:5-8). It's a new life. The second thing is a "living hope" (1:3). Because Jesus is alive, we have real hope, not just fairy tales to help us get to sleep at night. No matter what happens in this world, we can have the solid assurance that someday we'll be with Jesus forever.

Because of that, we should be "strangers" to the evil ways of this world (2:11). Instead, we should focus on living self-controlled, loving, and holy lives (1:13-16,22), even if we have to suffer or if everything goes wrong. And we can always rejoice because the Big Story has a happy ending for all who believe in Jesus Christ, and nothing can change that (1:4). In the meantime, we gain strength and support from knowing that we are part of the church—not a building, but "a people belonging to God" (2:9-10) with the living Christ as our leader. The Good News is that Jesus makes hope possible.

APPLY

What makes you sure about your faith? What makes you the most hopeful in life? How are your answers demonstrated in your actions?

PRAY

Lord, may the joy of my salvation and my commitment to follow you with all my heart be evident to everyone I meet...

Reading 94

JUST DO IT!

PRAY

Help me today, Lord, as I look intently into Your Word. I want to experience the blessing of doing what you say to me...

READ JAMES 1–2.

REFLECT

If Peter was a fighter and Paul was a thinker, James was a doer. He was also the brother of Jesus and the leader of the early church in Jerusalem (Acts 15:13-21). The main focus of his letter was to describe the practical aspects of what it means to be a Christian.

As we have seen, first-century Christians were experiencing persecution. So James's practical advice was to view these trials not as a reason to complain, but as an opportunity to grow (1:2-4). He had his finger on an important truth: Often the thing that causes us to grow the most in our walk with Christ is a time of crisis because it forces us more than anything else to depend on God. That doesn't mean you should go looking for trouble, but when it happens, rejoice! God has given you an opportunity to grow.

James also had some practical things to say about words. His advice sounds like the book of Proverbs—"be quick to listen, slow to speak and slow to become angry" (1:19; see also 1:26; James 3:1-12). What would happen if you spent an entire day trying to listen more than speaking? James also suggested a practical approach to the Word of God: It's good to reflect on it, but it's better to act on it (1:22-25).

Perhaps the most famous quote from this letter is "Faith without deeds is dead" (2:26). It would be easy to misunderstand what James meant. It's not that faith is unimportant or that doing good things is what God cares about most. The Bible is very clear that we can't earn our salvation (Ephesians 2:8-9). What James is saying is that if your faith is real, it must show up in your actions. If you were unable to speak, would others know you were a follower of Jesus?

APPLY

Make a list of the things you do that demonstrate the reality of your faith to others. What could you add to the list?

PRAY

Lord God, I'm so thankful for the truth of your Word. Give me a willingness and passion to do what it says...

Reading 95

AUTHENTIC CHRISTIANITY

PRAY

Heavenly Father, I thank you for loving me. Lord Jesus, I thank you for saving for me. Holy Spirit, I thank you for living in me...

READ 1 JOHN 3:11–4:21.

REFLECT

"I'm not sure when I became a Christian." Some people worry too much about that issue, others not enough. The important thing is to know that you are following Jesus now. So what are the marks of a true Christian? The apostle John offers us three essentials.

The first is to *believe in Jesus Christ* (3:23). That's the foundation of authentic Christian faith. And believing means at least two things: it's *agreeing* that Jesus is who he said he was, the risen Son of God, and then *following* his commands. Once you've decided to take those steps, nothing can separate you from the love of God (Romans 8:31-39).

The second mark of true Christians is that we've received *the Holy Spirit* (4:13). There is a lot of controversy about the work of the Holy Spirit in the church today. Some want to limit his work, perhaps as a reaction to those who overemphasize his work. But the New Testament is clear that the Holy Spirit is not something extra or just for a select few. He's here and available to all Jesus' followers (Acts 2:14-21,38).

The third mark of a true Christian is to *love others* (3:11,23; 4:21). John was blunt on this point (3:15; 4:7-8), but so was Jesus (John 15:12,17). And if you want to know what love is, think about what Jesus did. He gave his life for others (3:16). That's the highest possible standard of love. You may not be called on to become a martyr, but John was saying that Christian love involves sacrifice.

John knew what authentic Christianity was all about because he had been with Jesus. And he gave us this eyewitness report so we could have the assurance of knowing him too (1 John 1:1-4).

Apply

When have you ever given or received sacrificial love? Is there evidence of authentic Christianity in your life?

Pray

Lord Jesus, I believe that you are the living Son of God. Empower me by your Spirit to follow you with my whole heart... *

---

* Now turn to the Review Journal beginning on page 253 to record your key insights from the last five readings.

The Revelation

Revelation is a challenging book and is perhaps the most popular and most studied of the prophetic books in the Bible. People sometimes refer to it as The Revelation of Saint John, but that can be a little misleading because, in fact, it is the revelation of Jesus Christ (Revelation 1:1). John was simply the recipient who wrote it down for us to read.

From the very beginning John established that this was a message from God about the future (Revelation 1:1-3). The way God revealed that message was through a series of seven visions while John was on the island of Patmos (Revelation 1:9).

The first vision pertained to the early church, around A.D. 81–96. It had been approximately fifty years since Jesus had ascended into heaven, and the church was beginning to drift away from the gospel. Not only were Christians facing persecution, but they were also beginning to accept false teaching and adopt sinful patterns of behavior. You'll find the messages to the seven churches (Revelation 2–3) fairly easy to understand and very relevant to today.

The subsequent visions about the end of the world are more challenging to understand. Some people have tried to figure out the meaning of every detail in these visions, but that can be confusing at best. You might find it more helpful to reflect on the main themes from these visions, the way you do when you try to remember a dream you've had at night.

Probably the biggest theme running through the last chapters of Revelation is the final showdown between good and evil, between God and Satan. The descriptions are very dramatic, but the bottom line is that Satan is defeated. The visions also give us a picture of what heaven will be like. Again, our natural curiosity will make us want to get the exact picture of what it will be like. But the truth is, it will be even better than we can imagine. Why? Because the main feature of heaven is that all those who believe in Jesus will be with him forever.

One last thought before you complete your journey through the Bible: Don't let this be the end of your Bible-reading experience. Let it become the beginning of a lifetime dialogue with God. Once you've decided to become a follower of Jesus Christ, the best way to sustain and grow your relationship with him is to meet him daily in the Bible and prayer. (If you'd like information on how to receive more Bible-reading help, see page 276.)

Thanks for walking with me through the essential one hundred passages of the Bible!

Reading 96

A VOICE AND A VISION

PRAY

Lord God, I come into your presence, desiring to worship you in spirit and in truth (John 4:24). As I do, please give me a deeper understanding of Jesus…

READ REVELATION 1.

REFLECT

Let's nail down the facts: The apostle John is probably ninety years old by this time, which means Jesus left the earth about fifty years earlier. John had been sent to the island of Patmos because of his witness for Jesus (1:9), but he didn't know what would happen next. So he devoted himself to worshiping God (1:10).

That's a good thing to do when you are unsure of what to do next in life. It's important to reconnect with God, especially when you don't have all the answers. True worship gives us a deeper conviction that God is present and in charge of every detail in our lives. That's a good reason to praise him.

Worship also leads to deeper insight. First, John got a better understanding of Jesus, the central figure in the vision (1:13). Jesus was dazzling and overwhelming, and he held the keys to death and hell (1:18). That's a powerful position. It reminds us that when he came to earth the first time, Jesus came as Savior. When he comes again, Jesus will come as Judge. A second insight John received during worship was a better understanding of

God's perspective on the church (1:11). But we'll hear more about that in our next reading.

As you read these verses, you may have thought, *I wish my relationship with God could be as real and personal as John's.* Notice the clues John gives us about his walk with God. We've already noted that he committed himself to wholehearted worship. In addition, he was obedient to the word of God (1:2,9), he focused on Jesus (1:2-8), he eagerly embraced the Holy Spirit (1:10), and he endured suffering (1:9). That's the prescription for a deeper walk with God.

APPLY

How would you describe your relationship with God? How is that seen in the way you worship him?

PRAY

Lord Jesus, you are the first and the last, the Living One, the Almighty. I worship and praise you from the depths of my heart...

Reading 97

GOOD NEWS, BAD NEWS

PRAY

Lord, the door of my heart is open to you. I want to hear your voice and enjoy close fellowship with you today...

READ REVELATION 2–3.

REFLECT

One thing stands out in this passage: Jesus really cares about the church. That's a sobering thought, especially when we think of some of the things that go on in churches today. But it also reminds us of the deeper reality of the church. Jesus is there, and he knows what's going on. Notice how many times he said, "I know..." (2:2,9,13,19; 3:1,8,15). This should prompt us to carefully and prayerfully reflect on everything we do in our churches.

So what did Jesus have to say to these seven churches? There are different variations, but the main theme contrasts congregations who were faithful in teaching and practice with those who were unfaithful. If you have time, make a grid of the seven churches on a sheet of paper. Then, next to each church, summarize what it was commended for and what it was criticized for. You'll get a pretty clear picture of what Jesus wants from his people.

Two churches received only praise (Smyrna and Philadelphia). And note what they were praised for: They were poor and weak (2:9; 3:8). It's a fact that when we are powerless, we are much more willing to depend on God's power.

That's the secret of an effective church. Contrast that to the church in Sardis. Their problem was they thought they were alive, when in fact they were dead (3:1). Jesus' definition of success is often very different from ours. His message to a "successful, dead church" was to go back to the basics of the gospel: obey and repent (3:3).

In a way this passage can seem harsh. No church could ever completely measure up to what Jesus wants. But the encouraging thing is that his discipline is a reflection of his love for the church...and for you and me (3:19; see also Proverbs 3:12; Hebrews 12:6,10). So take heart, Jesus wants a relationship with you (3:20), and he's willing to go to great lengths to have it (Romans 5:8).

APPLY

How do you think Jesus would feel about your church? What message might he have for your church—and for you?

PRAY

Lord Jesus, you are my first love. Forgive me for the times when I become lukewarm in my commitment. My heart's desire is to remain faithful and true to you...

Reading 98

MY HEAVENS!

PRAY

You are worthy, Lord God, to receive glory and honor and power, for you created all things, and by your will they were created and have their being...

READ REVELATION 4–7.

REFLECT

This was some dream! Twenty-four elders dressed in white, colored horses, creatures with wings and eyeballs, a great worshiping multitude, and more. You don't need special effects to make this passage come alive. Some have tried to determine exactly what every detail means. But for our purposes, it's more helpful to look at the big picture: This is a vision of heaven.

What's your picture of heaven? A common view is that heaven is a place in the clouds where people go after death to strum harps and watch their relatives below. Country music makes it sound as if the best thing about heaven is that we get to meet Mother and Dad. Maybe we will, but the best thing by far will be to meet Jesus. The Lamb of God is at the very center of heaven (5:6; 7:17). Nothing else compares to that.

Yet there are some ominous aspects to John's vision. For example, the way to heaven isn't always a sentimental journey; sometimes it involves suffering (6:9). Also, it seems as if things may get worse before they finally get better

(6:1-17). But for those who belong to the Lamb, the end becomes the beginning of a wonderful eternity with Jesus (7:15-17).

So what will we do in heaven? The book of Revelation highlights worship as the main activity. What else could you do in the presence of Jesus? And note the makeup of this spectacular worshiping community: "Every nation, tribe, people and language" (7:9) will be represented. The reason we should share the Good News with all people and welcome them into our churches is not to be politically correct. It's because that's what heaven will be like.

APPLY

Why do you want to go to heaven? If God said to you, "Why should I let you into heaven?" what would you say?

PRAY

Salvation belongs to you, Lord God. Praise and glory and wisdom and thanks and honor and power and strength be to you forever and ever. Amen!

Reading 99

WAITING ON THE OVERLOOK

PRAY

Hallelujah! For you, Lord God Almighty, reign over all creation. I rejoice and give you all the glory…

READ REVELATION 19–20.

REFLECT

Several years ago we took a family trip to Niagara Falls on the border between New York and Canada. Standing on the overlook at the very edge of the falls, we could see the deep water of the Niagara River as it picked up speed and went careening over the edge into a roaring abyss far below. This passage is like standing on an overlook at the end of the world. It describes the incredible, unstoppable power of God sending Satan and evil over the edge into the abyss.

Although there are many curious and intriguing details to this passage, the main point is that, in the end, evil will be defeated (19:11–20:10). It doesn't always look that way now, especially when we see some of the awful things that happen in our world. At times the devil may seem to have the upper hand. But the Bible assures us that he doesn't. He lost the decisive battle at the Cross. What a wonderful thing to know that Satan's doom is guaranteed.

Another reality of the end is judgment (20:11-15). That's what the Book of Life symbolized. Some people envision the final judgment like a big scale. If your good deeds outweigh your bad deeds, you get a ticket to heaven. But that's not what the Bible says. Only those who believe in Jesus will be saved (Acts 10:43; Romans 10:9; 1 John 5:13).

For those who are in Christ, the end of the world will be a time of joy and celebration (19:1-10). The image John saw in his vision was that of a magnificent wedding with Jesus (the Lamb) as the groom and the church as his bride (19:7). Imagine what it will be like to stand on that overlook at the end of the world and be taken up to meet Jesus in the air. Hallelujah!

Apply

What words and emotions come to you when you think about the Final Judgment? Do you feel ready for it?

Pray

Jesus, I believe you are my Lord and Savior and that God raised you from the dead. I'm waiting on the overlook, with my hands held high in praise to you, for that wonderful day when you come to take me home...

Reading 100

THOSE PEARLY GATES

PRAY

"Your word, O LORD, is eternal; it stands firm in the heavens" (Psalm 119:89). Thank you so much, heavenly Father, for what you have taught me from my journey through the Bible...

READ REVELATION 21–22.

REFLECT

When our children were young, we had an illustrated edition of John Bunyan's classic allegory *The Pilgrim's Progress*. It's the story of a man named Christian who takes a journey from the City of Destruction through all kinds of dangers and temptations to the foot of the cross and finally to heaven. We read it at bedtime so many times that the binding finally wore out. Our children are grown now, but I still love to read that tattered book aloud. And whenever I get to the part where Christian enters the Celestial City, I still cry with joy. That's how I feel when I read this passage.

How can you express what it will be like to enter the gates of heaven? These two chapters are filled with what have become popular images of that wonderful moment—images such as pearly gates, streets of gold, and the River of Life. But as incredible as all that may sound, the reality of heaven is better still in two important ways.

First, everything will be new (21:5). Part of the curse of sin was that everything became subject to destruction and death (Romans 8:19-22). But when Jesus returns for his church, he will create a new heaven and a new earth (21:1), and a New Jerusalem will appear (21:2). Those are powerful images to describe how God will re-create his world. One joy of being a Christian is that you can be sure that one day your body, your life, your world, everything will all become gloriously new.

But the second and most important reality of heaven is that it is the place where the throne of God will be (22:3) and where he will dwell with his people forever (21:3). That was his plan from the very beginning, and it is why he sent his Son to earth (John 1:14). "For God so loved the world that he gave his one and only Son, that whoever believes in him shall not perish but have eternal life" (John 3:16). That's the Big Story of the Bible.

Apply

How do you feel when you think of heaven? How does it affect the way you worship and the way you live now?

Pray

*Thank you, God, that someday there will be no more death or mourning or crying or pain, and I will worship you with all your saints in the New Jerusalem. Come, Lord Jesus!**

---

* Now turn to the Review Journal beginning on page 253 to record your key insights from the last five readings.

Review Journal

After each section of five readings, summarize your most significant insights and prioritize your main applications. Before you begin a new section, read through your previous Review Journal entries so that you'll be reminded of what God has been teaching you.

Review: In the Beginning

Summarize your most significant insights from **In the Beginning.**

Prioritize your main applications from **In the Beginning.**

Review: Abraham, Isaac, and Jacob

Summarize your most significant insights from **Abraham, Isaac, and Jacob.**

Prioritize your main applications from **Abraham, Isaac, and Jacob.**

Review: The Story of Joseph

Summarize your most significant insights from **The Story of Joseph.**

Prioritize your main applications from **The Story of Joseph.**

Review: Moses and the Exodus

Summarize your most significant insights from **Moses and the Exodus.**

Prioritize your main applications from **Moses and the Exodus.**

REVIEW: THE LAW AND THE LAND

Summarize your most significant insights from **The Law and the Land.**

Prioritize your main applications from **The Law and the Land.**

REVIEW: THE JUDGES

Summarize your most significant insights from **The Judges.**

Prioritize your main applications from **The Judges.**

Review: The Rise of Israel

Summarize your most significant insights from **The Rise of Israel.**

Prioritize your main applications from **The Rise of Israel.**

Review: The Fall of Israel

Summarize your most significant insights from **The Fall of Israel.**

Prioritize your main applications from **The Fall of Israel.**

Review: Psalms and Proverbs

Summarize your most significant insights from **Psalms and Proverbs.**

Prioritize your main applications from **Psalms and Proverbs.**

Review: The Prophets

Summarize your most significant insights from **The Prophets.**

Prioritize your main applications from **The Prophets.**

Review: The Living Word

Summarize your most significant insights from **The Living Word.**

Prioritize your main applications from **The Living Word.**

Review: The Teachings of Jesus

Summarize your most significant insights from **The Teachings of Jesus.**

Prioritize your main applications from **The Teachings of Jesus.**

Review: The Miracles of Jesus

Summarize your most significant insights from **The Miracles of Jesus.**

Prioritize your main applications from **The Miracles of Jesus.**

Review: The Cross of Christ

Summarize your most significant insights from **The Cross of Christ.**

Prioritize your main applications from **The Cross of Christ.**

Review: The Church Is Born

Summarize your most significant insights from **The Church Is Born.**

Prioritize your main applications from **The Church Is Born.**

Review: The Travels of Paul

Summarize your most significant insights from **The Travels of Paul.**

Prioritize your main applications from **The Travels of Paul.**

Review: Paul to the Churches

Summarize your most significant insights from **Paul to the Churches.**

Prioritize your main applications from **Paul to the Churches.**

Review: Paul to the Leaders

Summarize your most significant insights from **Paul to the Leaders.**

Prioritize your main applications from **Paul to the Leaders.**

REVIEW: THE APOSTLES' TEACHING

Summarize your most significant insights from **The Apostles' Teaching.**

Prioritize your main applications from **The Apostles' Teaching.**

Review: The Revelation

Summarize your most significant insights from **The Revelation.**

Prioritize your main applications from **The Revelation.**

How to Discover a Lifetime Relationship with God

As you've discovered in this guide, the Big Story of the Bible is that God created a way for you to be free of your sin and to have a real relationship with him. That way is Jesus Christ.

As the apostle John wrote at the end of his gospel, "These are written that you may believe that Jesus is the Christ, the Son of God, and that by believing you may have life in his name" (John 20:31). Putting your faith in Jesus is the only way to have a relationship with God. It is also the way to enjoy the benefits of the new life God offers you in Christ. Here's what it involves:

- *Eternal life.* Jesus conquered death and came back to life. He gives life that lasts forever to everyone who has faith in him: "For God so loved the world that he gave his one and only Son, that whoever believes in him shall not perish but have eternal life" (John 3:16).
- *Meaningful life.* Jesus said, "I came so that everyone would have life, and have it in its fullest" (John 10:10, CEV). God wants your life to be fulfilling, and Jesus can give you both purpose and fulfillment.
- *Guilt-free life.* All of us have done things that are wrong. The Bible calls this sin, and sin separates us from God. But God offers us forgiveness through Jesus Christ. The apostle John wrote in his first letter, "But if we confess our sins to God, he can always be trusted to forgive us and take our sins away" (1 John 1:9, CEV).
- *New life.* "But to all who believed him and accepted him, he gave the right to become children of God" (John 1:12, NLT). God created us to have a special, close relationship with him, just as a child has with a loving parent. This new relationship with God is available to you through Jesus.

How Can I Have Faith in Jesus?

Having a new and living relationship with God may sound attractive to you. But, you may ask, How do I have faith in Jesus? Faith in Jesus is:

- *Admitting* that I can't get to heaven or have new life on my own because I have sinned and my sins have separated me from God.
- *Believing* that Jesus is the Son of God who died on the cross to pay for my sins and give me new life.
- *Deciding* to follow Jesus for the rest of my life.

Here's a simple prayer that you or a friend might say to God to tell him that you would like to receive the gift of new life offered by Jesus, his Son:

Dear God, I admit that I've done wrong things and that my sin has separated me from you. I believe you sent Jesus to earth to die for the sins of the world—including mine—and that you brought him back to life again. Lord Jesus, as of right now, I'm deciding to follow you every day. Holy Spirit, I ask for your help to live a new life. Amen!

About Your New Life

Living life the way God intended you to—to its fullest—means a daily relationship with him and with others who have new life in Christ. Here are some things that God wants us to do to make our relationships grow:

- *Talk to God.* That means prayer. You can talk to God anytime, either silently or aloud. God wants to hear from you. You can tell him what you think about him, thank him for what he's done, and ask him to provide for your needs or the needs of others around you.
- *Listen to God.* The main way God talks to us is through his book, the Bible. Reading the Bible can help you get to know God better and understand how he wants you to live. After you have completed *The Essential Bible Guide,* you can get more help in reading, understanding, and applying the Bible from other resources and books.

- *Join others who follow Jesus.* The Christian life is not just "a personal thing." God wants you to join other followers of Jesus. The best place to do that is in a church where the people love Jesus and believe the Bible. There you can find a place to belong, to serve and be served, and to grow in your relationship with God.
- *Tell others.* When you get a great new gift, you want to tell other people. Go ahead; share the best gift in the world—Jesus Christ. Don't be pushy. Just tell people what God has done in your life and trust him do the rest.

May God bless you!

The Essential 100 Challenge

Can you read the one hundred greatest passages from the world's most important book?

The Essential Bible Guide is based on one hundred carefully selected passages from the Old and New Testaments—The Essential 100—as shown below. Some groups, particularly churches and youth groups, could use these passages as the basis for an event to encourage Bible reading. The event, called "The Essential 100 Challenge," could take many forms, such as a public reading of The Essential 100, a congregation-wide campaign to read The Essential 100 together, or even a youth group fund-raiser, where the youth are sponsored to read The Essential 100 over a weekend. The Essential 100 Challenge can become a fun and positive way to raise the profile of the Bible in your church and community.

In the Beginning

1. Genesis 1–2
2. Genesis 3
3. Genesis 6:5–7:24
4. Genesis 8:1–9:17
5. Genesis 11:1-9

Abraham, Isaac, and Jacob

6. Genesis 12
7. Genesis 15
8. Genesis 21:1–22:19
9. Genesis 27–28
10. Genesis 32–33

The Story of Joseph

11. Genesis 37
12. Genesis 39–41
13. Genesis 42
14. Genesis 43–44
15. Genesis 45:1–46:7

Moses and the Exodus

16. Exodus 1–2
17. Exodus 3:1–4:17
18. Exodus 6:28–11:10
19. Exodus 12:1-42
20. Exodus 13:17–14:31

THE LAW AND THE LAND

21. Exodus 19:1–20:21
22. Exodus 32–34
23. Joshua 1
24. Joshua 3–4
25. Joshua 5:13–6:27

THE JUDGES

26. Judges 2:6–3:6
27. Judges 4–5
28. Judges 6–7
29. Judges 13–16
30. Ruth 1–4

THE RISE OF ISRAEL

31. 1 Samuel 1–3
32. 1 Samuel 8–10
33. 1 Samuel 16:1–18:16
34. 1 Samuel 23:7–24:22
35. 2 Samuel 5–7

THE FALL OF ISRAEL

36. 2 Samuel 11:1–12:25
37. 1 Kings 2–3
38. 1 Kings 8:1–9:9
39. 1 Kings 16:29–19:18
40. 2 Kings 25

PSALMS AND PROVERBS

41. Psalm 23
42. Psalm 51
43. Psalm 103
44. Proverbs 1–4
45. Proverbs 16–18

THE PROPHETS

46. Isaiah 51–53
47. Jeremiah 1:1–3:5
48. Daniel 6
49. Jonah 1–4
50. Malachi 1–4

THE LIVING WORD

51. John 1:1-18
52. Luke 1
53. Luke 2:1-40
54. Luke 3:1-20
55. Matthew 3:13–4:17

THE TEACHINGS OF JESUS

56. Matthew 5:1–6:4
57. Matthew 6:5–7:29
58. Matthew 13
59. Luke 10:25-37
60. Luke 15

THE MIRACLES OF JESUS

61. Luke 9:1-36
62. Matthew 14:22-36
63. John 9
64. Mark 5:1-20
65. John 11

THE CROSS OF CHRIST

66. Luke 22:1-46
67. John 18
68. John 19
69. John 20–21
70. Acts 1:1-11

THE CHURCH IS BORN

71. Acts 2
72. Acts 3–4
73. Acts 6:8–8:8
74. Acts 8:26-40
75. Acts 10:1–11:18

THE TRAVELS OF PAUL

76. Acts 9:1-31
77. Acts 13–14
78. Acts 15
79. Acts 16–20
80. Acts 25–28

PAUL TO THE CHURCHES

81. Romans 8
82. Galatians 5:16–6:10
83. Ephesians 6:10-20
84. Philippians 4:2-9
85. Colossians 1:1-23

PAUL TO THE LEADERS

86. 1 Timothy 3
87. 1 Timothy 6:3-21
88. 2 Timothy 2
89. 2 Timothy 3:10–4:8
90. 1 Thessalonians 4:13–5:11

THE APOSTLES' TEACHING

91. 1 Corinthians 13
92. 2 Corinthians 4:1–6:2
93. 1 Peter 1:1–2:12
94. James 1–2
95. 1 John 3:11–4:21

THE REVELATION

96. Revelation 1
97. Revelation 2–3
98. Revelation 4–7
99. Revelation 19–20
100. Revelation 21–22

For Further Study

If you enjoyed this Fisherman Resource, you might want to explore our full line of Fisherman Resources and Bible Studyguides. The following books offer time-tested Fisherman inductive Bible studies for individuals or groups.

Fisherman Resources

The Art of Spiritual Listening: Responding to God's Voice Amid the Noise of Life by Alice Fryling
Balm in Gilead by Dudley Delffs
Questions from the God Who Needs No Answers: What Is He Really Asking of You? by Carolyn and Craig Williford
Reckless Faith: Living Passionately as Imperfect Christians by Jo Kadlecek
Soul Strength: Spiritual Courage for the Battles of Life by Pamela Lau

Fisherman Bible Studyguides

Topical Studies

Angels by Vinita Hampton Wright
Becoming Women of Purpose by Ruth Haley Barton
Building Your House on the Lord: A Firm Foundation for Family Life (Revised Edition) by Steve and Dee Brestin
Discipleship: The Growing Christian's Lifestyle by James and Martha Reapsome
Doing Justice, Showing Mercy: Christian Action in Today's World by Vinita Hampton Wright
Encouraging Others: Biblical Models for Caring by Lin Johnson
The End Times: Discovering What the Bible Says by E. Michael Rusten
Examining the Claims of Jesus by Dee Brestin
Friendship: Portraits in God's Family Album by Steve and Dee Brestin

The Fruit of the Spirit: Growing in Christian Character by Stuart Briscoe
Great Doctrines of the Bible by Stephen Board
Great Passages of the Bible by Carol Plueddemann
Great Prayers of the Bible by Carol Plueddemann
Growing Through Life's Challenges by James and Martha Reapsome
Guidance & God's Will by Tom and Joan Stark
Heart Renewal: Finding Spiritual Refreshment by Ruth Goring
Higher Ground: Steps Toward Christian Maturity by Steve and Dee Brestin
Images of Redemption: God's Unfolding Plan Through the Bible by Ruth E. Van Reken
Integrity: Character from the Inside Out by Ted W. Engstrom and Robert C. Larson
Lifestyle Priorities by John White
Marriage: Learning from Couples in Scripture by R. Paul and Gail Stevens
Miracles by Robbie Castleman
One Body, One Spirit: Building Relationships in the Church by Dale and Sandy Larsen
The Parables of Jesus by Gladys Hunt
Parenting with Purpose and Grace by Alice Fryling
Prayer: Discovering What Scripture Says by Timothy Jones and Jill Zook-Jones
The Prophets: God's Truth Tellers by Vinita Hampton Wright
Proverbs and Parables: God's Wisdom for Living by Dee Brestin
Satisfying Work: Christian Living from Nine to Five by R. Paul Stevens and Gerry Schoberg
Senior Saints: Growing Older in God's Family by James and Martha Reapsome
The Sermon on the Mount: The God Who Understands Me by Gladys M. Hunt
Speaking Wisely: Exploring the Power of Words by Poppy Smith
Spiritual Disciplines: The Tasks of a Joyful Life by Larry Sibley
Spiritual Gifts by Karen Dockrey
Spiritual Hunger: Filling Your Deepest Longings by Jim and Carol Plueddemann
A Spiritual Legacy: Faith for the Next Generation by Chuck and Winnie Christensen

Spiritual Warfare by A. Scott Moreau
The Ten Commandments: God's Rules for Living by Stuart Briscoe
Ultimate Hope for Changing Times by Dale and Sandy Larsen
When Faith Is All You Have: A Study of Hebrews 11 by Ruth E. Van Reken
Where Your Treasure Is: What the Bible Says About Money by James and Martha Reapsome
Who Is God? by David P. Seemuth
Who Is Jesus? In His Own Words by Ruth E. Van Reken
Who Is the Holy Spirit? by Barbara H. Knuckles and Ruth E. Van Reken
Wisdom for Today's Woman: Insights from Esther by Poppy Smith
Witnesses to All the World: God's Heart for the Nations by Jim and Carol Plueddemann
Women at Midlife: Embracing the Challenges by Jeanie Miley
Worship: Discovering What Scripture Says by Larry Sibley

Bible Book Studies

Genesis: Walking with God by Margaret Fromer and Sharrel Keyes
Exodus: God Our Deliverer by Dale and Sandy Larsen
Ruth: Relationships That Bring Life by Ruth Haley Barton
Ezra and Nehemiah: A Time to Rebuild by James Reapsome
(For Esther, see Topical Studies, *Wisdom for Today's Woman*)
Job: Trusting Through Trials by Ron Klug
Psalms: A Guide to Prayer and Praise by Ron Klug
Proverbs: Wisdom That Works by Vinita Hampton Wright
Ecclesiastes: A Time for Everything by Stephen Board
Song of Songs: A Dialogue of Intimacy by James Reapsome
Jeremiah: The Man and His Message by James Reapsome
Jonah, Habakkuk, and Malachi: Living Responsibly by Margaret Fromer and Sharrel Keyes
Matthew: People of the Kingdom by Larry Sibley
Mark: God in Action by Chuck and Winnie Christensen
Luke: Following Jesus by Sharrel Keyes

John: The Living Word by Whitney Kuniholm
Acts 1–12: God Moves in the Early Church by Chuck and Winnie Christensen
Acts 13–28, see *Paul* under Character Studies
Romans: The Christian Story by James Reapsome
1 Corinthians: Problems and Solutions in a Growing Church by Charles and Ann Hummel
Strengthened to Serve: 2 Corinthians by Jim and Carol Plueddemann
Galatians, Titus, and Philemon: Freedom in Christ by Whitney Kuniholm
Ephesians: Living in God's Household by Robert Baylis
Philippians: God's Guide to Joy by Ron Klug
Colossians: Focus on Christ by Luci Shaw
Letters to the Thessalonians by Margaret Fromer and Sharrel Keyes
Letters to Timothy: Discipleship in Action by Margaret Fromer and Sharrel Keyes
Hebrews: Foundations for Faith by Gladys Hunt
James: Faith in Action by Chuck and Winnie Christensen
1 and 2 Peter, Jude: Called for a Purpose by Steve and Dee Brestin
1, 2, 3 John: How Should a Christian Live? by Dee Brestin
Revelation: The Lamb Who Is the Lion by Gladys Hunt

Bible Character Studies

Abraham: Model of Faith by James Reapsome
David: Man After God's Own Heart by Robbie Castleman
Elijah: Obedience in a Threatening World by Robbie Castleman
Great People of the Bible by Carol Plueddemann
King David: Trusting God for a Lifetime by Robbie Castleman
Men Like Us: Ordinary Men, Extraordinary God by Paul Heidebrecht and Ted Scheuermann
Moses: Encountering God by Greg Asimakoupoulos
Paul: Thirteenth Apostle (Acts 13–28) by Chuck and Winnie Christensen
Women Like Us: Wisdom for Today's Issues by Ruth Haley Barton
Women Who Achieved for God by Winnie Christensen
Women Who Believed God by Winnie Christensen

About the Author

WHITNEY T. KUNIHOLM has been the president of Scripture Union/USA since 1997. Prior to working with Scripture Union, Whitney was the executive vice president for Prison Fellowship Ministries near Washington, D.C., a ministry in which he served in a variety of roles for more than thirteen years.

Whitney has written seven books on the subject of personal and group Bible study, including two Fisherman Bible Studyguides—*Galatians, Titus, and Philemon: Freedom in Christ* and *John: The Living Word.* He has also written articles for newsletters and Christian magazines.

Whitney and his wife, Carol, live in Exton, Pennsylvania. He is actively involved in the prayer and small-group ministry of his church and occasionally preaches and teaches there. Whitney and Carol have three children: Stephanie (in high school), Matthew (in college), and Anna (an artist, who is married to Steve).

About Scripture Union

Scripture Union/USA began in 1959 and is committed to "helping people meet God every day." Today Scripture Union conducts evangelism and discipleship programs for children, youth, and families in various locations across the country. In addition, Scripture Union produces a variety of Bible-reading publications for all ages.

Scripture Union/USA is headquartered in Valley Forge, Pennsylvania, and is a charter member of the Evangelical Council for Financial Accountability (ECFA). In addition, Scripture Union/USA is part of a worldwide fellowship of Scripture Union ministries in more than 130 countries.

For many years Christian leaders have realized the importance and effectiveness of Scripture Union's ministry and materials:

"I am totally, completely, and forever a Scripture Union man."
—Billy Graham

"I heartily endorse this ministry." —Jill Briscoe

"Scripture Union taught me the discipline of daily Bible reading—a discipline I consider indispensable to Christian growth and freshness."
—John Stott

Scripture Union welcomes your interest, prayers, and support.

Scripture Union/USA
P.O. Box 987, #1
Valley Forge, PA 19482
Phone: 1-800-621-LAMP
Web Site: www.ScriptureUnion.org

MORE BIBLE READING HELP

If you enjoyed using *The Essential Bible Guide,* then you'll want to try *Discovery,* the quarterly guide that helps you find practical help from the Bible every day. To receive a free issue, call Scripture Union at 1-800-621-LAMP.

Discovery takes you through the Bible in a four-year cycle in which you read about ten to twenty verses each day. *Discovery* uses the same five-step method that you experienced in *The Essential Bible Guide*—Pray, Read, Reflect, Apply, Pray. In addition, *Discovery* has many special features to help you grow: weekly topical studies for individuals or groups, a through-the Bible-in-one-year schedule, extra resources to enrich your study of God's Word, plus an opportunity to receive *DiscoveryDirect: The Daily Email Bible Guide.* To sign up, go to www.BibleReadingCenter.com.